Seashore

of
Southern
California

Written and Illustrated by
Ian Sheldon

© 2007 by Lone Pine Publishing International Inc.
First printed in 2007 10 9 8 7 6 5 4 3 2 1
Printed in China

The Distributor: Lone Pine Publishing

1808 B Street, Suite 140
Auburn, WA 98001
USA

Website: www.lonepinepublishing.com

Library and Archives Canada Cataloguing in Publication

Sheldon, Ian, 1971-
    Seashore of southern California / written and illustrated
    by Ian Sheldon.

Includes bibliographical references and index.
ISBN-13: 978-1-55105-232-8

1. Seashore biology--California, Southern--Identification.
2. Seashore biology--California--Pacific Coast--Identification.
I. Title.

HQ95.7.S445 2007   591.769'9097949   C2006-904417-1

Cover Illustration: Nine-toothed Pebble Crab by Ian Sheldon
Illustrations: Ian Sheldon
Image Scanning: Elite Lithographers

PC: P14

To Roger,

For shared vision and spirit

Or something.

CONTENTS

Speckled Scallop

CONTENTS

ACKNOWLEDGEMENTS

I am grateful to my parents for exposing me to so many different parts of the world and the natural features of those places. Through them I have obtained a broad appreciation and recognition for the beauty and diversity of the natural world.

I will never forget the brilliance of Dr. Peter Grubb, a man who welcomed me into Cambridge University and who saw an ecologist and naturalist in me, a path from which I very nearly strayed.

I wish to extend my thanks to the staff at Lone Pine Publishing, to the editorial department and to the production team, both of which are a pleasure to work with. Eloise Pulos and Lee Craig make the editorial process a dream. The outstanding design work of Rob Weidemann and Jau-Ruey Marvin for this series of seashore guides has resulted in books that are both beautiful and artistic. I am grateful to Lone Pine Publishing for the opportunity to write and illustrate a book on this environment, about which I feel so passionately. On this note, I would like to acknowledge all the hardworking and pioneering scientists who have increased and shared their knowledge about the West Coast, so that we can all share in its wonders.

Blue and Gold Nudibranch

Sea Otter
to 5' • p. 31

California Sea Lion
to 8' • p. 32

Northern
Elephant Seal
to 16' • p. 33

Pacific Harbor Seal
to 16' • p. 34

Black Prickleback
to 12" • p. 35

Longjaw
Mudsucker
to 8" • p. 36

Rockpool Blenny
to 6.75" • p. 37

Wooly Sculpin
to 7" • p. 38

Roughjaw Frogfish
to 13.5" • p. 39

Island Kelpfish
to 4" • p. 40

Blackeye Goby
to 6" • p. 41

Blue-banded Goby
to 2.5" • p. 42

Northern Clingfish
to 6" • p. 43

Plainfin
Midshipman
to 15" • p. 44

Opaleye
to 26" • p. 45

Grass Rockfish
to 22" • p. 46

Garibaldi
to 14" • p. 47

Reef Surfperch
to 7" • p. 48

California Grunion
to 7.5" • p. 49

California
Moray
to 5' • p. 50

FISHES

Round Stingray
to 22' • p. 51

White-cap Limpet
to 10' • p. 52

Fingered limpet
to 1.25' • p. 53

Rough Limpet
to 1.25" • p. 54

LIMPETS

Shield Limpet
to 1" • p. 55

Giant Owl Limpet
to 4.5" • p. 56

Volcano Limpet
to 1.5" • p. 57

Great Keyhole
Limpet
to 5" • p. 58

SNAILS

Onyx Slipper Shell
to 2" • p. 59

Spiny Cup-and-
Saucer Shell
to 2" • p. 60

Black Abalone
to 6" • p. 61

Black Tegula
to 1.75" • p. 62

Checkered
Periwinkle
to 2.75" • p. 63

Banded Turban
to 1" • p. 64

Wavy Turban
to 6" • p. 65

Lewis's Moonsnail
to 5.5" • p. 66

Norris's Topshell
to 2.25" • p. 67

Angled Unicorn
to 1.5" • p. 68

Gem Murex
to 1.75" • p. 69

Western Mud
Whelk
to 24.5" • p. 70

Joseph's Coat
Amphissa
to 0.75″ • p. 71

Giant Western
Nassa
to 2″ • p. 72

Emarginate
Dogwinkle
to 1″ • p. 73

Poulson's
Rock Shell
to 2″ • p. 74

Festive Murex
to 2.75″ • p. 75

Giant Forreria
to 6″ • p. 76

Three-winged
Murex
to 3″ • p. 77

Tinted Wentletrap
to 0.6″ • p. 78

Cooper's Turret
to 2.25″ • p. 79

Ida's Miter
to 3″ • p. 80

California Cone
to 1.5″ • p. 81

Large
Coffee Bean
to 0.5″ • p. 82

Chestnut Cowry
to 2.5″ • p. 83

Purple Dwarf Olive
to 1.25″ • p. 84

Striped Barrel
Snail
to 0.75″ • p. 85

California
Paper Bubble
to 2″ • p. 86

Speckled Scallop
to 3.5″ • p. 87

Giant Rock Scallop
to 10″ • p. 88

Clear Jewel Box
to 3.5″ • p. 89

False Pacific
Jingle Shell
to 4″ • p. 90

BIVALVES

Native Pacific
Oyster
to 3.5" • p. 91

California
Mussel
to 8" • p. 92

Blue Mussel
to 4" • p. 93

California
Jack-knife Clam
to 4.25" • p. 94

Bean Clam
to 1" • p. 95

Common
Pacific Egg
to 1.25" • p. 96

Bent-nosed
Macoma
to 3" • p. 97

California Mactra
to 2" • p. 98

Pismo Clam
to 7" • p. 99

Sunset Clam
to 4" • p. 100

Common
Pacific Littleneck
to 3" • p. 101

Common
Washington Clam
to 4.75" • p. 102

Wavy Chione
to 2" • p. 103

Pacific Gaper
to 9" • p. 104

Nuttall's Cockle
to 5.5" • p. 105

Little Heart Clam
to 0.5" • p. 106

Pacific Shipworm
to 0.25" • p. 107

Merten's Chiton
to 2" • p. 108

Lined Chiton
to 2" • p. 109

Mossy Chiton
to 3.5" • p. 110

California
Nuttall's Chiton
to 2" • p. 111

Conspicuous
Chiton
to 4.5" • p. 112

Yellow-edged
Cadlina
to 3" • p. 113

Ring-spotted
Doris
to 3.5" • p. 114

Opalescent
Nudibranch
to 3" • p. 115

Elegant Aeolid
to 3.5" • p. 116

Sea Clown
Nudibranch
to 6" • p. 117

Blue and Gold
Nudibranch
to 2.5" • p. 118

Orchid Nudibranch
to 1.5" • p. 119

Hopkin's Rose
to 1.25" • p. 120

Navanax
to 8" • p. 121

Brown Sea Hare
to 20" • p. 122

Two-spotted
Octopus
to 36" • p. 123

Opalescent Squid
to 12" • p. 124

Bat Star
to 8" • p. 125

Ochre Star
14" • p. 126

REFERENCE GUIDE

SEA STARS

Giant Sea Star
to 24″ • p. 127

Short-spined
Sea Star
to 24″ • p. 128

Six-rayed Sea Star
to 3.5″ • p. 129

Blood Star
to 8″ • p. 130

Panamanian
Serpent Star
to 20″ • p. 131

Spiny Brittle Star
to 15″ • p. 132

Eccentric
Sand Dollar
to 3.25″ • p. 133

SEA URCHINS

SEA CUCUMBERS

Red Sea Urchin
to 5″ • p. 134

Purple Sea
Urchin
to 3.5″ • p. 135

Dwarf Sea
Cucumber
to 1″ • p. 136

Warty Stichopus
to 10″ • p. 137

JELLYFISH

Purple-striped
Pelagia
to 32″ • p. 138

Sea Gooseberry
to 1″ • p. 139

By-the-wind Sailor
to 4″ • p. 140

ANEMONES & CORAL

Aggregating
Anemone
to 3.5″ • p. 141

Giant Green
Anemone
to 10″ • p. 142

Proliferating
Anemone
to 2″ • p. 143

Club-tipped
Anemone
to 1.25″ • p. 144

White-spotted
Rose Anemone
to 4" • p. 145

Orange Cup Coral
to 0.4" • p. 146

Yellow Crab
to 7" • p. 147

Swimming Crab
to 3" • p. 148

Striped Shore Crab
to 2.5" • p. 149

Shield-backed
Kelp Crab
to 4.75" • p. 150

Nine-toothed
Pebble Crab
to 3.75" • p. 151

Lumpy Pebble Crab
to 1.5" • p. 152

Porcelain Crabs
to 1" • p. 153

California
Fiddler Crab
to 0.75" • p. 154

Blue-handed
Hermit Crab
to 0.75" • p. 155

Pelagic Red Crab
to 2" • p. 156

California Spiny
Lobster
to 30" • p. 157

Acorn Barnacle
to 0.6" • p. 158

Giant Acorn
Barnacle
to 4" • p. 159

Volcano Barnacle
to 2" • p. 160

Red-striped
Acorn Barnacle
to 2" • p. 161

Blue Goose
Barnacle
to 2.75" • p. 162

Leaf Barnacle
to 3.25" • p. 163

Red Rock Shrimp
to 2.75" • p. 164

REFERENCE GUIDE

SMALL CRUSTACEANS

Smooth Skeleton
Shrimp
to 2" • p. 165

Harford's Greedy
Isopod
to 0.75" • p. 166

Western
Sea Roach
to 1" • p. 167

California
Beach Flea
to 1.1" • p. 168

WORMS

Tapered Flatworm
to 2.5" • p. 169

Green
Nemertean
to 20" • p. 170

Eighteen-scaled
Worm
to 4" • p. 171

Clam Worm
to 6" • p. 172

Red Tube Worm
to 4" • p. 173

Scaly Worm Shell
to 5" • p. 174

Sand Castle Worm
to 2" • p. 175

Giant Feather
Duster
to 11" • p. 176

OTHER SMALL ORGANISMS

Kelp Encrusting
Bryozoan
variable • p. 177

Rosy Bryozoan
variable • p. 178

Ostrich Plume
Hydroid
to 4" • p. 179

Purple Sponge
to 36" • p. 180

Velvety Red
Sponge
to 36" • p. 181

Sea Pork
to 8" • p. 182

Monterey Stalked
Tunicate
to 2.75" • p. 183

Yellow-green
Sea Squirt
to 6" • p. 184

Feather Boa
to 15' • p. 185

Oar Weed Kelp
to 5' • p. 186

Giant Perennial
Kelp
to 7.5" • p. 187

Bull Kelp
to 80' • p. 188

Rockweed
to 20" • p. 189

Sargassum
to 6' • p. 190

Tar Spot
to 8" • p. 191

Sea Staghorn
to 16" • p. 192

Enteromorpha
Green Algae
to 10" • p. 193

Sea Lettuce
to 20" • p. 194

Nail Brush
to 3" • p. 195

Turkish Towel
to 18" • p. 196

Iridescent Algae
to 36" • p. 197

Coralline Algae
to 4" • p. 198

Encrusting Coral
variable • p.199

Surf Grass
to 6" • p. 200

Eelgrass
to 36" • p. 201

Blobs of Tar
variable • p. 202

Introduction

The temptations are always there—a beautiful coast, some rocks, some tide-pools. For most of us, a walk along the beach or a holiday on the coast brings many joys. What child could resist picking up that strange stringy seaweed cast ashore by the waves, or peering into a rocky tide-pool and giggling at the shy hermit crabs? For some of us, the curiosity lives with us always.

Purple Sponge

The shoreline is incredibly diverse, from extensive sandy beaches to vertical cliffs, from craggy rocks to quiet bays. In all these different landscapes, wildlife abounds. The wonderful thing about this environment is that it gives us, terrestrial animals that we are, a chance to glimpse into the ocean, a world with which we are not familiar. As the tide recedes, creatures are exposed and many of them bear no resemblance to those on land. Is it a plant or animal? Maybe it is just a piece of rock. Maybe something lives in it. There are many amazing mysteries waiting to be uncovered, waiting to be solved.

As you walk towards the shore, smell the sweetness of the sea, feel the salty spray against your skin and sway to the soothing motion of the waves washing back and forth. Remember that you are on the edge of another world. Let yourself go and discover some of the secrets of our coasts and the creatures within. The rewards are tremendous.

About This Book

Lined Chiton

No trip to the coast or wind-swept walk along a beach is complete without a nature guide to identify just what it is you are looking at. Secrets abound, and while you might know that you are holding a sand dollar, do you really know what a sand dollar is and what it does with its life? This book is an easy guide to help you discover some of the stories behind the strange objects and animals found along the coasts of Southern California.

Included in the guide are some of the plants and animals that you are likely to encounter as you gaze into a tidepool or wade through an eelgrass meadow. This guide is by no means exhaustive. If you had all the guides to everything you might encounter, you would probably need a truck to carry them. This book covers the plants and animals you will commonly see as you wander and wonder through the intertidal zone: you will find information about shells, sea lions, anemones, urchins, squids, seaweeds, fishes and so much more. If birds are your passion, many other guides specifically deal with these feathered friends.

Nine-toothed Pebble Crab

17

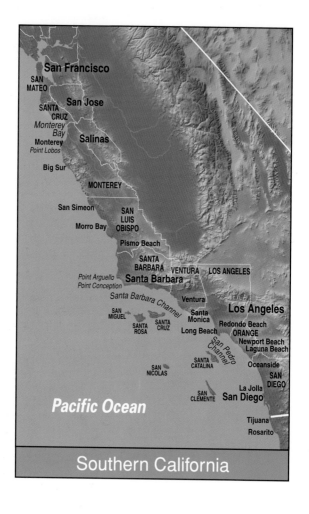

San Francisco

SAN MATEO

San Jose

SANTA CRUZ

Monterey Bay

Salinas

Monterey

Point Lobos

Big Sur

MONTEREY

San Simeon

SAN LUIS OBISPO

Morro Bay

Pismo Beach

SANTA BARBARA

VENTURA

LOS ANGELES

Point Arguello

Point Conception

Santa Barbara

Santa Barbara Channel

Ventura

Santa Monica

Los Angeles

SAN MIGUEL

SANTA ROSA

SANTA CRUZ

Redondo Beach

ORANGE

Newport Beach

Laguna Beach

Long Beach

San Pedro Channel

SANTA CATALINA

Oceanside

SAN NICOLAS

SAN DIEGO

La Jolla

SAN CLEMENTE

San Diego

Pacific Ocean

Tijuana

Rosarito

Southern California

Cooper's Turret

How to Use This Guide

At the front (pp. 7–15) is a quick reference guide to all the groups and primary species covered by this book. The reference guide will allow you to make a visual assessment of the object of your interest. The 18 groups are identified with color bars to help you find the correct section of the book.

Each species is given a whole page with an illustration or two, text about the plant or animal and a small text box covering some of the basics, including 'Other Names,' scientific and common, given to the species. First, check that the creature resembles the one illustrated. If you are unsure, refer to the inset box and check some of the information given here. 'Range' tells you where it occurs in California, as well as in other states. 'Zone' (described shortly) refers to its position on the shore. 'Habitats' describes the types of places that the creature enjoys, perhaps the tidepools or maybe muddy sand, for example. The creature's dimensions are given so you can determine if it is the right size—maximum sizes are given; bear in mind that all things are born small and grow larger.

Spiny Brittle Star

If the animal you are watching is green, but the illustration is red, check 'Color' in the inset box to see if it comes in different colors; many of the creatures you will encounter adapt to their environment, taking on different colors for camouflage. If you are still not satisfied, some entries have a 'Similar Species' category, referring you to other species in the book that look the same. Some similar species are also written about in the main text.

Read about the object of your fascination, and discover some of its stories as well as facts about its curious biology. Where possible, the use of strange and long scientific words has been avoided. One or two sneak their way in, and a glossary at the back (pp. 203–06) will help you if the terms don't make sense.

The California Coast

The coastline of California is very diverse, from steep cliffs on exposed shores, to the quiet waters of the bays. Some areas are estuarine, where fresh water mixes with salty. Sandy beaches stretch into the distance and look so tempting.

The range covered by this guide is chiefly Southern California, from Point Conception to the Mexican border. Many of the species will occur beyond these boundaries, but only the range north of the Mexican border is described for each entry. If you have ever tried swimming off Southern California's gorgeous beaches, you know how cold the water can be. The reason for such chilly seas is that the California Current, a large offshore mass of water, moves gently southwards, bringing cold water from the far north. East of the Channel Islands, however, the current is not so significant, and a smaller current sometimes moves north-wards. The water close to the shore has a chance to warm up during summer months, and these warmer temperatures permit creatures from Mexico to take up residence in Southern California. This warmer water means that the marine life of Southern California can be quite different from Northern and Central California, although many of the species do occur throughout the state. Point Conception is generally the northern limit for many of the warmth-loving creatures—north of the Point the water is just too cold.

Once in a while 'El Niño' influences the waters along the Pacific Coast. During an El Niño year (roughly once every four or more years), the ocean currents move north instead of south, bringing warm waters from the tropics. In turn, this change in water temperature brings many different animals into the area, changing the local ecology for a time. Some of the creatures included in this book are species found in California only during these warmer years.

Giant Green Anemone

Tides & the Intertidal Zone

Every coastline is shaped in some way by the tides. Two times a day the tide rises and falls. It seems remarkable that an ocean as enormous as the Pacific can move so much water around. Where does all the water go?

Clam Worm

Both the moon and the sun are tugging at the oceans. Just as our planet has the power to attract objects, the moon and the sun do, too. The moon is closer but smaller than the sun. When the moon and sun are aligned, they both tug at the oceans, pulling the water to the side of the planet nearest them. Thus, when the tide rises in one part of the world, it is dropping somewhere else. A perfect alignment of the moon and sun creates the greatest rise and fall of the ocean. The most dramatic change in sea level along the West Coast occurs in Puget Sound, Washington, with up to a 20-foot difference between high and low tide. Just exactly how much the tide will rise and fall depends on the exact position of the sun and moon.

This constant motion of the sea up and down a beach creates distinct zones for wildlife. Near the high-tide line, plants and animals must tolerate long periods out of water, while those at the low-tide line require long periods underwater. Some creatures and seaweeds are very particular about which part of the beach they will live in. To help you identify an animal or plant, the inset box has an entry for the 'Zone' in which it is found. Several zones are described:

Spray or Splash Zone—the uppermost part of the beach influenced by wave action. Here, the rocks only ever receive splashes from the surf or spray, and are never covered by the sea.

Feather Boa

21

Upper Intertidal Zone—the uppermost band covered by the highest point of an incoming tide. Here, organisms must tolerate prolonged periods exposed to the elements.

Middle Intertidal Zone—the middle band covered half the time by the tides. More organisms are able to survive here, because they are not exposed to drying conditions for too long.

Lower Intertidal Zone—the lowest part of the beach that is only uncovered for a short period of time. Here, growth is luxuriant, because many organisms can tolerate the short exposure to air.

Often included under 'Zone' are the terms **'inshore'** and **'open water,'** where inshore means that the creature will come close to the shoreline, and open water means that they are usually out in the seas far from the shore.

The high-tide line is the highest point that the sea will reach on the incoming tide; the low-tide line is the point at which the sea is as far out as it will go. Once the tide reaches its lowest point, it begins to come in, or rise, again. Below the low-tide line is the **Subtidal Zone**, which is never exposed by a receding tide. The sealife in this zone can be very different because it is never exposed to the rigors of the air, sun or rain or the presence of beachcombers.

Red Sea Urchin

Dwarf Sea Cucumber

Club-tipped Anemone

Beachcombing
What to Do and What Not to Do

So much fun is to be had from beachcombing, but there are a number of important points to remember to ensure that it is a success and pleasure for you and for those who come after you.

Choosing the right location is a good start. While all coastlines will have their wildlife, some will be better than others. Gently sloping, rocky beaches riddled with tidepools are perhaps the most rewarding. But don't count out wading through an eelgrass meadow, or hiking the fringes of a quiet bay either. Safety is a concern—you don't want to fall off a cliff, be swept away by a large wave or get stuck in estuarine mud when the tide starts to come in.

Be very wary of the tides, and learn how to read the tide tables that are posted in national parks and at information offices in ports and towns. Tide tables will help you decide what time of day to go to the beach—aim for an ebb tide, because it is safer to follow the water receding out to the low-tide line, than to be chased back up the beach by a rising tide. Where the shore is very flat the tide can race in, cutting you off on a rocky ledge or sand bar. Be vigilant!

Some organisms, such as the California Mussel (p. 92), thrive where the surf is strongest and waves pound the shores, and these organisms are useful indicators of 'crazy surf.' Freak waves do happen, and they take their victims from time to time. Don't be one of them. It is very easy to become so engrossed in a tidepool that you lose all sense of

Pelagic Red Crab

time and place, and before you know it, the tide is rushing in with full force. With this caution in mind, beachcombing is best done in a group in case of accidents, and also because your treasured finds can be more enjoyable when shared with others.

The treasures of beachcombing come small and large. Bring a pail and a hand lens to study the small creatures. Some of these creatures will only emerge from their homes when underwater. A hand lens will help you see the tiny animals that make up a bryozoan colony, for example. And bring this book! It will help you identify and learn about the shore.

Many people believe that they can take some of their finds home. First, think about where you are—removal is forbidden in many locations—and know the local laws and regulations. Second, think about the luckless victim of your interest. Many sea stars have been transported home in the hope that they will dry and make eye-catching souvenirs. They don't. They rot, they smell bad and you kill them. Similarly, don't transfer organisms to fresh water—that will kill them, too. In short, resist the temptation to take anything. The rocky tidepool is the home for shorelife, and the creatures would probably rather stay there.

Many plants and animals of the ocean are considered fine eating. If you are tempted to try them out, never harvest every one in sight. Too many creatures have succumbed to overharvesting. It is important to check local regulations regarding the sizes of shellfish that are harvested—most have a minimum size requirement to meet before they can be collected. Also, check for information about 'red tide,' which poisons some shellfish, and if you eat them you might well regret it. If you want to harvest some seaweed, don't pull up the whole plant, just trim off part of the plant so that it can still grow and reproduce.

24

Bat Star

Most important of all, respect the shoreline. It is not yours. You do not own the wildlife on it. Living creatures deserve your love and attention; try not to interfere. Do turn over rocks to see what is hiding underneath, and do put these rocks back the way you found them, in their original position so the animals feel protected once more. Watch out for creatures as you clamber about the rocks. It is tempting to use mussel and barnacle beds for good footing on steep rocks. Each step you take will kill. A small chip off a mussel shell opens it up to the elements and to predation.

Beaches make popular locations for picnics. Make sure you take all your garbage home with you. Plastic waste is hazardous to wildlife and broken glass might end up in the foot of the next beachcomber that follows you. Don't just take your own garbage home with you, but remove what other people have left behind. Sadly, our oceans have long been seen as giant refuse pits, with tons of garbage cast from ships. This garbage floats ashore in its various forms, sometimes dangerous, always ugly.

Shorelife to Discover

The shorelife of the intertidal zone comes in so many shapes and sizes that an overview of each group might help you understand where they fit in with the natural order of things. Some animals look so strange you would be forgiven for thinking that they are plants!

There are animals with backbones (vertebrates), there are animals without backbones (invertebrates) and there are seaweeds (plants). The few vertebrates you will discover are the fishes and mammals, but by far the majority of the creatures you will encounter are the invertebrates. The invertebrates covered in this guide fall into distinct groups: mollusks, echinoderms, cnidarians, crustaceans, worms and other small organisms.

Blue-banded Goby

Orchid Nudibranch

Mollusks

The largest group covered by this guide is the mollusks, and it includes some very different organisms indeed. It is hard to believe, for example, that a massive octopus is related to a limpet stuck on a rock. A mollusk is typified by a soft body and a hard shell for protection (though some mollusks have lost this shell). Lining the internal side of the shell is soft tissue called the 'mantle,' and this mantle creates a cavity in which gills for breathing are located. There are distinct groups of mollusks: limpets and snails (the gastropods); bivalves; chitons (the polyplacophorans); sea slugs (the nudibranchs, also gastropods); and squids and octopus (the cephalopods).

Gastropods have one large sucking foot and a shell of various forms. The nudibranchs are also gastropods, but they have lost their shell and rely on other means to protect themselves. The bivalves are all the clams, oysters and scallops. They are grouped together because they all have two valves, or shells, which enclose the soft body of the animal, and a muscular foot often used for burrowing. The polyplacophorans are limpet-like with their huge sucking foot, but they have a line of eight separate articulating plates down the back. The least likely looking mollusks are the squids and octopus, called cephalopods. Highly intelligent and active, they are the most advanced of all the mollusks.

The dietary preferences of mollusks are as varied as their forms. Some mollusks graze on microscopic algae; some snails ferociously prey on other snails; squids grapple with lively prey; and bivalves, which are filter feeders, suck water into the mantle cavity to sift it for tiny particles.

Echinoderms

'Echinoderm' means 'spiny skin,' and this group of animals is strictly marine. It includes the sea stars, brittle stars, sea urchins and sea cucumbers. These creatures are ancient animals of pre-historic times, and are still very successful today. They have radial symmetry, usually based on the form of a five-pointed star. Seawater is pumped around the body to hydraulically power the tiny tube feet that move the animals around. Their firm structure is given by a calcareous skeleton most obvious in dead sea urchins, such as the Eccentric Sand Dollar (p. 133). Echinoderms have the remarkable ability to regenerate limbs. A spine can regrow on an urchin, and a whole leg can grow back on a sea star—however, this ability does not give you license to go pulling them to pieces!

Short-spined Sea Star

Cnidarians

Cnidarians are the soft, jelly-like animals of the sea. They include the jellyfish, sea anemones and corals. They are typified by having stinging tentacles to capture their prey. The sting comes from the tiny cells, called 'nemato-cysts,' lining the tentacles. Corals are soft-bodied animals that lay down a calcareous base to which they attach. It is the coral 'skeletons' that make up the elaborate reefs in tropical waters. Hydroids resemble extremely small colonies of corals and occur in many different forms. This guide has only one species of coral.

Proliferating Anemone

Shield-backed Kelp Crab

Crustaceans

These animals have jointed limbs and hard outer skins, or shells. They are a very successful group, and are best represented by the crabs. Shrimps, barnacles and beach fleas are also crustaceans, however, and their enormously diverse forms are reflected in the many different lifestyles and eating habits. Having a tough outer skeleton has a distinct disadvantage—how do you grow? Crabs, for example, have overcome this growth problem by molting periodically. They lose the old, hard skin for a new, more flexible one that gradually hardens. Molting is a dangerous time for crustaceans, because their usually tough outer skin momentarily becomes soft and vulnerable. The cast-off skeletons of crabs frequently wash ashore in great numbers.

Worms

Most of the worms in this guide are annelid worms. These segmented creatures have many appendages that assist in walking and breathing. Some wander and are ferocious predators, while others, such as Red Tube Worms (p. 173), stay put, build a tube around themselves and filter the water with a pretty fan of feather-like appendages on the head. Other worms featured include the Green Nemertean (p. 170), which is a very different kind of worm, not related to the annelids. Nemerteans do not have distinct segments, but have one long, stretchy body. The Tapered Flatworm (p. 169) belongs to another group of worms called the platyhelminths. These flatworms can spread themselves so thinly that they all but disappear.

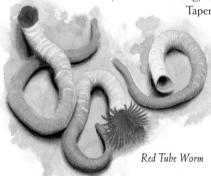

Red Tube Worm

Other Small Organisms

There are many other less distinct groups to be found along the seashore. These groups include the bryozoans, poriferans and urochordates.

Bryozoans, sometimes called moss animals, are so small that they can be missed or mistaken for something else. Bryozoans are tiny colonial animals that build walled homes of calcium carbonate about them. As the colony expands, it takes on a distinctive form particular to the type of bryozoan. There are many different kinds, and colonies can be shaped like trees, bushes and flat encrustations or grow convincingly as corals. They are filter feeders, using tentacles that extend from their little homes.

Poriferans are simple sponges. They are animals represented by loose aggregations of cells organized to filter water and extract the tiny particles of food from it. Usually, the surface of a sponge is covered in tiny pores through which water passes in and out. Typically, a sponge grows flat in the intertidal zone, but in deeper, calmer water it can be much more elaborate and grows to great sizes. Many sponges have tiny silica strands to serve as a skeleton, or support. These small crystals are often used by nudibranchs when they have been ingested.

Urochordates are peculiar animals that actually bear some resemblance and connection to humans—for at least part of their lives. They are classified in the same large group as us, the chordates, but have gone off in their own direction in evolutionary terms. When they are very young and free swimming, they have gills, a little tail and a nerve cord running down their back. They somewhat resemble tadpoles or humans, when we are first developing as embryos. Soon all that changes, and what looks like it is going to be an advanced and extraordinary animal, loses all these features, settles down on a rock and becomes a strange blob of flesh that filters water throughout its life. They can be solitary or live in colonies, and are called sea squirts or tunicates.

Ostrich Plume Hydroid

Seaweeds

The plants of the inter-
tidal zone come in various shapes
and sizes, and have been classified
accordingly. There are four
groups to consider. Algae are divided into
three principal groups: brown, green and
red. The fourth group, the flowering
plants, is only represented by a few
grass-like plants in the sea. Collectively,
these algae and flowering plants are commonly known as seaweeds.

Bull Kelp

Algae

The larger family of brown algae includes
the magnificent kelps. Their color is determined by
the dominant pigments for harnessing the energy
from the sun (photosynthesis), and they usually come
in shades of brown, although some retain rich olive-green
colors. The kelps are very successful, forming huge forests
just offshore.

The green algae family includes the fleshy, green algae
of the intertidal zone. The dominant pigments used in
photosynthesis make the algae green. Some are very bright
green, while others can be so dark they appear to be black.

Just to confuse the issue of classification, the red algae
family can come in shades of red, brown, green or blue. In
addition, some have incorporated calcium carbonate into
their structures, taking on hard and crusty coralline forms.
Some of the red algae can be very beautifully and richly colored, and the exact color they have depends on the balance
of the pigments used in photosynthesis.

Flowering Plants

Do not expect to find a sunflower or geranium, but look
out for grass-like plants growing in quiet bays or on rocky
shores. These are Eelgrass (p. 201) and Surf Grass (p. 200).
They are flowering plants like
those on land, with a root system and neat rows of inconspicuous flowers tucked in
close to the stem. For pollination,
they rely on the sea to carry pollen
from one flower to the next, just in
the same way as terrestrial grasses
rely on the wind.

Surf Grass

Sea Otter
ENHYDRA LUTRIS

Little surpasses the beauty of a playful and intelligent Sea Otter baby nestled on the furry belly of its floating mother. The Sea Otter was once persecuted to the point of extinction, and its thick pelt, vital for chilly waters, made it a popular animal for trapping. Now protected and making a strong recovery, the Sea Otter is a cherished sight for wildlife watchers—Monterey Bay is one of the best places to observe it—and its presence is evidence of a healthy ecosystem. Point Conception appears to mark the dividing line for the Sea Otter; females can be seen with pups to the north of the point, while to the south sighted otters are frequently wandering males. Introductions have been made on San Nicolas Island with limited success. Watch out for the River Otter (*Lutra canadensis*), with its longer tail and slimmer build, which also occasionally takes to the seas.

Five feet long and needing copious quantities of fuel to keep warm, the Sea Otter has a voracious appetite for shellfish, crabs, urchins and fishes. When the Sea Otter had all but been annihilated, sea urchin populations grew so large that the kelp forests were being overgrazed. With the otter now returning, the kelp forests are healthy and balanced once again. Fisheries still fear the otter's huge appetite, and although protected by law, the Sea Otter can be a sad victim of oil spills—the fur's waterproof and insulating qualities are destroyed when oil seeps into it.

RANGE: California, Washington, British Columbia, Alaska; scattered

ZONE: inshore; occasionally on shore

HABITATS: kelp beds

LENGTH: 5 ft

WEIGHT: 100 lb

California Sea Lion

ZALOPHUS CALIFORNIANUS

Fun-loving performers, California Sea Lions are bold and sometimes daring. They are commonly used in marine aquariums to perform tricks; in the wild, they take delight in flinging kelp around and bodysurfing in large waves. They often mix with other seals and sea lions at haul-outs on sandy beaches, flat reefs and rocky shores. Sea lion beach parties are often quite raucous—their loud barks can be heard from afar.

RANGE: Southern California to British Columbia

ZONE: intertidal to open water

HABITATS: rocky shores; beaches

LENGTH: male to 8 ft; female to 6.5 ft

WEIGHT: male to 750 lb; female to 250 lb

Female California Sea Lions stay year-round at their favored breeding grounds on the Channel Islands in Southern California, but the males move as far north as Canada after breeding. These sea lions have black, hairless flippers that help them swim swiftly and dive to the impressive depths of 800 feet in their quest for fish and squid.

The California Sea Lion resembles the less common Steller Sea Lion (*Eumetopias jubatus*), but is darker and smaller, and the male has a prominent ridge on his forehead, a feature lacking in the Steller Sea Lion. Steller Sea Lions are more reserved about barking and are a rare sight south of Point Conception.

Northern Elephant Seal

MIROUNGA ANGUSTIROSTRIS

Aside from beached whales, the Northern Elephant Seal is the largest mammal a beachcomber is likely to encounter. Massively intimidating, this hefty beast gets its name from the male's extended snout. In December, the huge males and comparatively tiny females begin to come ashore to breed, a time when the male's snout is grossly inflated. Males try to impress one another, scarring each other's chest and neck in the process. In California the breeding grounds of these spectacular animals include the Channel and Farallon islands. One of the best mainland sites to witness them is in Año Nuevo State Park in San Mateo County.

In summer months, after breeding, the males migrate northwards in search of rich feeding and a place to molt. During the molting season, they are seen lounging around on rocky shores and islands, seldom doing much at all. Occasional sightings are made in quiet inland waters, but they prefer open seas, where they can dive to staggering depths of 5000 feet for an hour or more. They feed on fishes, squids, octopuses and even the occasional shark! Once almost wiped out by over-hunting for their oily skin, these seals have since made a dramatic recovery.

RANGE: Southern California to Alaska

ZONE: intertidal to open water

HABITATS: rocky shores; isolated beaches

LENGTH: male to 16 ft; female to 9 ft

WEIGHT: male to 5000 lb; female to 2000 lb

Pacific Harbor Seal

PHOCA VITULINA

These pretty harbor seals are mammals that are commonly seen close to human activity. Found from the open coast into protected bays as well as estuaries and up rivers, they have the confidence to enter harbors and swim beside boats, while curiously observing the contents. Pacific Harbor Seals come in a variety of colors from white to black, the most common combination being a buff color flecked with darker spots.

When the tide is in, they are actively diving and hunting, eating all manner of fishes. They are partial to the occasional clam or squid. At low tide they haul out onto rocky platforms to sunbathe, where they can be seen singly or in groups. Pacific Harbor Seals always have one eye open for humans who approach too close. When afraid, the seals readily dive into water.

OTHER NAME: Leopard Seal

RANGE: California to Alaska

ZONE: intertidal to open water

HABITATS: rocky shores; beaches; estuaries; harbors

LENGTH: male to 6 ft; female to 5.5 ft

WEIGHT: male to 300 lb; female to 175 lb

Underwater, however, they are in their element, and can be quite curious and friendly with divers. They make themselves unpopular with fishermen, unfortunately, because they cunningly steal fishes from nets. They are, in turn, the prey of Orcas (killer whales) and even suffer the hungry attentions of the Northern Elephant Seal (p. 33).

Black Prickleback

XIPHISTER ATROPURPUREUS

Chocolate-brown or black, this lithe, eel-like fish has some distinctive markings on its face, which help us to identify it. Two comical, black bands descend from the eye and are bordered in white. The similar Rock Prickleback (*X. mucosus*) has eye bands that are pale and bordered in black. These two fish occur together in Santa Barbara County; only the Black Prickleback is found south of Santa Barbara. At the base of the tail, most Black Pricklebacks have a white band. The pectoral fin just behind the gills is so small as to be hardly noticeable.

Black Pricklebacks are common fish when the tide is out. Larger ones will tend to hide under rocks, while the younger, smaller pricklebacks can be seen in tidepools. Be careful when turning over rocks because several males might be underneath, all wrapped around their egg masses. Be especially careful when placing the rock back where it was. The males patiently wait up to three weeks for the eggs to hatch. Some land animals, such as garter snakes and feisty minks, will come down at low tide to dine on these sheltering pricklebacks.

OTHER NAME: Black Blenny
RANGE: Southern California to Alaska
ZONE: lower intertidal; subtidal to 25 ft
HABITATS: tidepools; under rocks; rocky shores
LENGTH: to 12 in
COLOR: dark red-brown to black

Longjaw Mudsucker

GILLICHTHYS MIRABILIS

If you are a beachcomber perusing the muddy banks of estuaries, sloughs and quiet bays, then the Longjaw Mudsucker will be one of the most likely fishes you will encounter. Be sure to peep into small burrows where it might have retreated for cover. Because of its preference for intertidal muddy areas, this fish is frequently stranded in shallow pools as the tide goes out. In such situations, it is more than happy to slither its way across the mud to another pool. Their darkly mottled backs help these fishes blend into the mud they enjoy. Mudsuckers are easy to catch out of water. Longjaw Mudsuckers have been widely used as sportfishing bait, and they are less common now than before.

RANGE: Southern and Central California
ZONE: intertidal
HABITATS: tidal flats; bays; estuaries; sloughs; mud bottoms
LENGTH: to 8 in
COLOR: brown; mottled

The most distinctive feature of this fish is the huge mouth, with an upper jaw extending as far back as the gills. When breeding males defend their territories, they open and inflate their mouths as much as possible. You might think that a pair doing so are kissing, when actually they are shoving each other around to show which male is the stronger—the loser will quietly move away leaving the successor to his patch of mud.

Rockpool Blenny

HYPSOBLENNIUS GILBERTI

A common resident of pools is the Rockpool Blenny. This blenny is a master of disguise with its mottled brownish colors. If you are poking about in a tide-pool, be sure to brush your hand through some seaweed to see if you can flush a blenny or two out of hiding. The Rockpool Blenny is unique for its hairy cirrus above the eye, which somewhat resembles an elaborate eyebrow. Beneath the eye there are usually some dark-colored bands stretching down to the chin. This blenny gets its other common name of 'Notchbrow Blenny' from the distinctive depression behind the eye.

Blennies will most often be darting around low-intertidal pools filled with crevices and some seaweed. Here, they will be chipping away at limpets, bryozoans, algae and anything else that takes their fancy. If removed from their home tide-pool and placed in another pool, you can be fairly sure that after the next high tide Rock-pool Blennies have found their way back to their original pool. Tidepools are more usually filled with the similar Wooly Sculpin, which has two separate dorsal fins. The Bay Blenny (*H. gentilis*) is also similar, but lacks the hairy cirrus and notch behind the brow, and will often be sporting a bright red chin.

OTHER NAME: Notchbrow Blenny

RANGE: from Point Conception south

ZONE: lower intertidal; subtidal to 60 ft

HABITATS: rockpools; rocky shores

LENGTH: to 6.75 in

COLOR: brown, olive; mottled

SIMILAR SPECIES: Wooly Sculpin (p. 38); Island Kelpfish (p. 40)

Wooly Sculpin
CLINOCOTTUS ANALIS

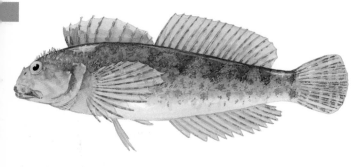

One of the tidepool's most entertaining features is surely the innumerable small fishes darting about and resting here and there on colorful rocks and seaweeds. In Southern California, you can be fairly sure that these small fishes are Wooly Sculpins. In central and northern regions, they are more likely to be smooth Tidepool Sculpins (*Oligocottus maculosus*). The Wooly gets its name from many tiny, hairy growths, called 'cirri,' projecting from around the head. Most often these sculpins are gray-green, with darker saddles along the back and cream or pinkish markings along the side. They will adapt their color to the dominant colors in their favorite pool, so, for example, look for reddish Woolies in reddish tidepools.

RANGE: Southern and Central California

ZONE: intertidal; subtidal to 60 ft

HABITATS: tidepools; rocky and gravel shores

LENGTH: to 7 in

COLOR: gray-green, reddish, brown; cream or pink markings

SIMILAR SPECIES: Rockpool Blenny (p. 37)

Near the high-tide line, you will find younger Wooly Sculpins. Older fish prefer the pools in the middle to lower intertidal zones, where occasionally they can grow to lengths of 7 inches. Once a maturing sculpin has found a favorite tidepool, it will return to the same spot at each low tide. Here, it will happily dine on just about any creature small enough to fit into its mouth, including crabs. Another similar resident of tidepools is the Rockpool Blenny, but this fish has one long continuous dorsal fin instead of two.

Roughjaw Frogfish

ANTENNARIUS AVALONIS

The Roughjaw Frogfish is just so ugly it is borderline cute. Resembling an irregular sponge, this fish looks clumsy and oafish. It is, however, a master of surprise and patience. This globular fish gently moves about until it finds a suitable crevice or hole into which it can squish its body. The fish will adapt its color to match the surrounding rocks and seaweeds. This camouflage, coupled with a mass of prickles and protrusions on its own body, helps it blend in with its environment almost perfectly.

The Roughjaw Frogfish is usually missed by beachcombers, but it attracts the attentions of smaller fish. Between the eyes and on the end of a little rod is an 'esca,' or lure. The fish can wiggle the rod back and forth, making the esca look like a tiny animal. A hungry fish might well approach anticipating a meal. When the fish is close enough, however, the frogfish rapidly opens its cavernous mouth and the smaller fish is swept in, all in the blink of an eye.

RANGE: from Santa Catalina Island and Orange County south

ZONE: intertidal; subtidal to 360 ft

HABITATS: tidepools; rocky shores

LENGTH: to 13.5 in

COLOR: gray, green, yellow, red, brown, black; mottled

Island Kelpfish

ALLOCLINUS HOLDERI

Common on the Channel Islands, from which it gets its common name, the Island Kelpfish is an attractive little fish found in tidepools and other rocky areas. This fish is often reddish, with thin, red lines running down its flanks and broad vertical and irregular bars along the back. The dorsal fin is very long, with two longer spines at the front end where there is a distinctive greenish patch. The dorsal fin is usually red and orange, with a pale border along the top. The greenish anal fin also has a paler border. The pectoral fins behind the gill are unusually long.

The Island Kelpfish is an accomplished color changer, which helps it adjust to and blend in with new habitats. If you are looking for kelpfish, poke about in seaweed in lower tidepools. If the seaweed is green, the camouflaged kelpfish will also be green. While you are roughing up some seaweed you are sure to come across some other types of fish, including blennies, which are similar in appearance (though often larger). Be sure to check that your Island Kelpfish isn't a Rockpool Blenny.

RANGE: from Santa Cruz Island south

ZONE: intertidal; subtidal to 162 ft

HABITATS: rocky shores; tidepools; seaweed

LENGTH: to 4 in

COLOR: reddish, variable

SIMILAR SPECIES: Rockpool Blenny (p. 37)

Blackeye Goby

CORYPHOPTERUS NICHOLSI

Lovely in pinks, tans and other pale colors, this small fish sports a number of distinguishing features. The large, dark eyes and black border to the first dorsal fin stand out against the pale body, which is covered in large scales. Just underneath the eye is a faint iridescent blue patch, and along the top of the head is a fleshy ridge. Breeding males have dark pelvic fins, the very sight of which can sometimes be enough to lure a female into a cave. Usually, however, it takes a bit of a dance to convince a female to enter a male's abode, where she then lays her eggs. After fertilization, the male guards the eggs until they hatch.

The best goby sites are where rocks and sand meet, because the male can excavate a burrow to his liking beneath a rock. He will courageously defend this site by puffing up his cheeks and looking large. If that fails, he can always retreat into the burrow for protection. Curiously, these feisty males started life as females, changing sex as they aged. Another goby that will also be seen darting into burrows (in this case, ones left by other animals) is the pale gray Arrow Goby (*Clevelandia ios*).

OTHER NAMES: Crested Goby; Bluespot Goby

RANGE: Southern California to Alaska

ZONE: lower intertidal; subtidal to 450 ft

HABITATS: tidepools; rocks and sand

LENGTH: to 6 in

COLOR: tan, brown, yellow, pink; sometimes speckled

Blue-banded Goby

LYTHRYPNUS DALLI

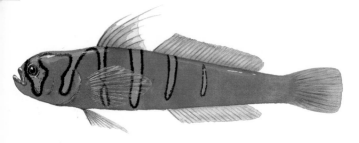

There is no mistaking a Blue-banded Goby when you see one. These are stunning little fishes: what they lack in size they make up for in color. Blue-banded Gobies occur in the intertidal zone, and you might be lucky to come across a stranded fish in a tidepool. Your best bet for seeing one, however, is to go diving, because they can be very abundant subtidally.

RANGE: from Morro Bay south
ZONE: intertidal; subtidal to 250 ft
HABITATS: rocky shores
LENGTH: to 2.5 in
COLOR: red; blue stripes

In case you do stumble across a stranded goby in a lower intertidal pool, they are bright red with four to nine dazzling blue stripes. With colors like that, it comes as no surprise that they want to be noticed. They sit atop rocks near a crevice, and will guard their territories. If you pose too much of a threat, then the feisty goby decides that cover is a better option, either in its crevice, or, very sensibly, between the elaborate armory of sea urchins.

Male Blue-banded Gobies have longer spines in the first dorsal fin than females. Curiously, these fishes can change their sex—female one season, male the next. Even though these fishes don't live very long at all (less than two years), they can certainly be very abundant in some years.

Northern Clingfish

GOBIESOX MAEANDRICUS

An oversized tadpole best describes this intertidal fish. The broad, flattened head and narrow, tapered body are very distinctive. Specially modified fins on the underside of the head allow the tenacious Northern Clingfish to suck onto the undersides of rocks in shallow water. Lift a rock gently and look at the underside to see if any clingfishes are hanging on for their lives. This fish's sucking disc is so effective that it can be a challenge to remove the fish from a rock. If you succeed, place it on the palm of your hand and hold it upside down—this fish really does cling!

The Northern Clingfish forages on other under-rock inhabitants, especially small crustaceans, mollusks and worms. The female lays a clutch of eggs on the underside of a rock, and the male will guard the eggs until they hatch. The color of a clingfish is variable, from light to dark browns and reds, with mottling and a pale bridge usually connecting the eyes. These fishes are more common north of Point Conception. South of the Point they share their range with the much smaller California Clingfish (*G. rhessodon*), which has similar coloration but is only 2.5 inches long. Both clingfishes are frequently overlooked because of their dark colors and habit of hiding under rocks.

OTHER NAME: Flathead Clingfish
RANGE: Southern California to Alaska
ZONE: intertidal; subtidal to 26 ft
HABITATS: under rocks and kelp
LENGTH: to 6 in
COLOR: variable red and brown; mottled

Plainfin Midshipman

PORICHTHYS NOTATUS

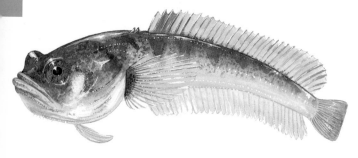

In late spring, male Plainfin Midshipmen take up temporary residence in the shallows, where they hum the night away. This strange buzz, croak or, at a real stretch of the imagination, song is made by the fish squeezing air around its swim bladder (a gas-filled organ that allows the fish to adjust its buoyancy). The female Midshipmen find this sound more attractive than do humans, and they search out the males to lay their eggs. The residents of Sausalito (San Francisco Bay) to the north know the sounds of the Plainfin Midshipman all too well—they find them quite distressing when they are trying to sleep.

This depressed-looking fish has many tiny light organs, or photophores, on its underside. These photophores will flash when the fish is handled, but their function might be for courtship or to light up the underside to make the fish look pale against the brighter light above. Perhaps it looks sad because just about everything seems to eat it—sea lions, birds, other fishes and many others dine on it, but remarkably, it is not so popular among fish-eating humans. The Plainfin Midshipman is active by night, preferring to remain buried by day, with its bulbous eyes poking through the muddy sand. Be sure to check near rocks at low tide in quiet bays for males protecting their egg masses.

OTHER NAMES: Northern Midshipman; Singing Toadfish

RANGE: Southern California to Alaska

ZONE: lower intertidal; subtidal to 1200 ft

HABITATS: bays; estuaries; under rocks

LENGTH: to 15 in

COLOR: green, brown or purplish

Opaleye
GIRELLA NIGRICANS

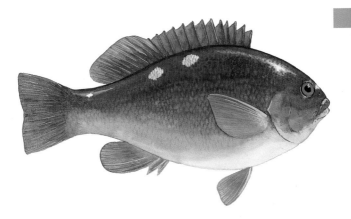

For at least a part of its life, the Opaleye will live in the tidepools of Southern California. Look for energetic juvenile Opaleyes, up to 4 inches in length, darting about in almost any tidepool. In smaller tidepools, the fishes might take to breathing air at the surface if they use up all the oxygen in the water. As they grow, the young Opaleyes will move into larger pools closer to permanent water.

For the very first part of their lives the bluish young swim free in the open ocean. As they age they turn greenish and move inshore, and the characteristic white spots develop on their backs. There are usually one or two of these spots. Once the young are about 4 inches in length they move back offshore into the subtidal waters, usually near kelp beds. As well as the spots, the Opaleye has a very distinctive bright blue eye, and some have a small, white bar across the nose. Adult Opaleyes are often brought ashore by pier anglers. A greenish Opaleye might be mistaken for the Grass Rockfish, which lacks the white spots.

OTHER NAME: Opaleye Perch

RANGE: from Central California south

ZONE: intertidal; subtidal to 100 ft

HABITATS: tidepools; kelp beds; rocky shores

LENGTH: to 26 in

COLOR: gray-green above; silvery below

SIMILAR SPECIES: Grass Rockfish (p. 46)

Grass Rockfish

SEBASTES RASTRELLIGER

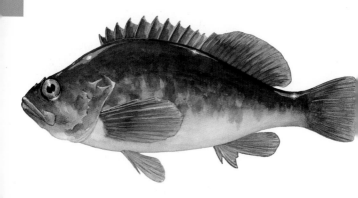

Just offshore, along rocky coastlines begins the world of the rockfishes. There are many different species of these chunky, spiny fish, but the one the beachcomber is likely to encounter is the Grass Rockfish. Dark green and mottled, this species is colored this way to help it blend in with kelp and eelgrass beds where it likes to hang out. In some fishes, the lower fins might be tinged with pink.

At low tide it is possible to see the Grass Rockfish in large tidepools. Another sure bet for a close encounter with one is to become friendly with an angler, because it is a popular fish to eat. Its tendency to hang out close to the shore makes it accessible to anglers, and its big size makes it worth the angler's effort. If a rockfish escapes these baited hooks, it can live to a reported 17 years, during which time it is dining on crabs, octopuses and other fishes. The sad-looking Plainfin Midshipman (p. 44) falls prey to the Grass Rockfish when it enters rockfish territory to spawn.

OTHER NAME: Grass Rockcod

RANGE: Southern California to Oregon

ZONE: lower intertidal; subtidal to 150 ft

HABITATS: tidepools; rocky shores

LENGTH: to 22 in

COLOR: mottled dark green

SIMILAR SPECIES: Opaleye (p. 45)

Garibaldi

HYPSYPOPS RUBICUNDUS

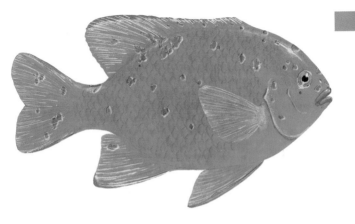

Deservedly, the magnificent Garibaldi is recognized as the state fish of California. Its size and orange brilliance make it one of the gems of the ocean. The Garibaldi is a member of the damselfish family, a tropical group filled with the most beautiful of fish. Adults, reaching some 14 inches in length, were an easy target of spear-fishermen, and their stunning looks made them popular for marine aquaria enthusiasts. Now they are fully protected by law.

The young are frequently found in tidepools, and are bright orange or red, with blue spots (as illustrated). When they reach about 6 inches in length, they lose the blue spots and move into deeper waters where they set up and defend their home territories. When defending against all manner of invaders, Garibaldis are known to emit loud clicking sounds, perhaps to alarm the intruders. Adults can be seen from rocky vantage points flashing their dazzling orange flanks as they swim to defend their home and nest. Although they can be seen as far north as Monterey Bay, they are common only south of Point Conception where the coast and ocean bottom is rocky.

RANGE: from Monterey Bay south
ZONE: intertidal; subtidal to 95 ft
HABITATS: tidepools; rocky shores
LENGTH: to 14 in
COLOR: adults bright orange; juveniles orange, with blue spots

Reef Surfperch
MICROMETRUS AURORA

This cheerful little fish can be commonly seen in the larger tidepools of Southern California and in the shallow subtidal waters of rocky shores as far north as Tomales Bay in Central California. Schools of Reef Surfperch gather in the rocky shallows near seaweeds, where they feed on algae and small invertebrates. Many fishes are in the same family as the Reef Surfperch, but this surfperch is one of the few that gets caught in large tidepools and swims near enough to the shore to be accessible to the curious beachcomber.

OTHER NAME: Reefperch

RANGE: Central and Southern California

ZONE: lower intertidal; subtidal to 30 ft

HABITATS: tidepools; rocky shores

LENGTH: to 7 in

COLOR: blue-green, silver; with black and gold markings

The coloring of this fish is typical of many fishes that don't want to be seen too easily. The back of the fish is blue-green so that it is hard for predators to detect the fish from above. Meanwhile, predators beneath the Reef Surfperch have a hard time seeing it because its belly is pale, to match the bright light from the surface. Distinctive markings on the Reef Surfperch include a bold splash of black behind each gill and pectoral fin, as well as a patch of black-edged scales along the lower sides. The large scales are further enhanced by a band of gold stretching almost from head to tail.

California Grunion

LEURESTHES TENUIS

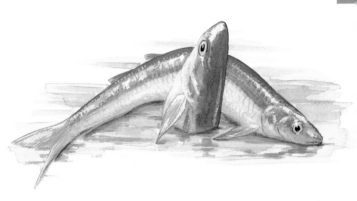

From March through August on nights when the moon is full and spring tide is at its highest, a strange phenomenon can be witnessed. On the sandy beaches of Southern California, the California Grunion comes ashore and crowds of people gather to watch. Driven by an urge to crawl out onto the beach to lay their eggs, these slippery, silvery fishes are brought in by the waves and remain on the sand where they dance and flip about.

The females bury themselves tail first into the moist sand, while the males wrap themselves against the females. This action allows the male's sperm to drain down the body of the female and fertilize the eggs deep in the sand where they are protected. Once the eggs have been laid and fertilized, these fishes leave with the next big wave. At the next high tide, the eggs hatch.

SPAWNING RANGE: from Monterey Bay south
ZONE: low-tide line; subtidal to 60 ft
HABITATS: sandy beaches; open ocean
LENGTH: to 7.5 in
COLOR: silvery-blue and green

With a strong desire to dine on these fishy creatures, people gather in great numbers to catch them, but also just to watch. Fortunately for this seething mass of fishes, the law dictates that anglers are only allowed to catch California Grunions with their bare hands. This restriction gives them some chance at returning to the open water just offshore.

California Moray

GYMNOTHORAX MORDAX

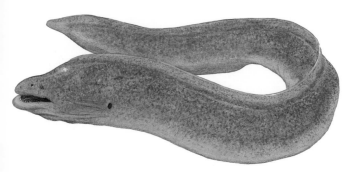

F ew fish have the evil reputation of the moray eels. But, like many ugly-looking beasts with teeth, their reputation is worse than the reality. The California Moray, reaching a length of 5 feet, and well armed with sharp, serrated teeth, will not actively pursue and bite a diver unless the diver has provoked it. So, don't go poking your hands down dark holes along rocky shores! The California Moray is not very common intertidally, but caution in large tidepools near the low-tide line should still be used.

RANGE: from Point Conception south

ZONE: intertidal; subtidal to 130 ft

HABITATS: rocky shores; caves; crevices

LENGTH: to 5 ft

COLOR: green, brown, variable; mottled

By day, it retreats into a crevice or cave with only its gruesome head poking out. By night, the eel emerges to forage, making a meal out of lobsters, crabs, fishes, and even rubbery octopuses and spiny sea urchins. Unlike other fishes, it lacks the pelvic and pectoral fins, and the gill opening is a small, round hole set back from the mouth. The California Moray is brown or greenish, with mottling. These eels are a common sight on the offshore islands, where they can live for as long as 30 years.

Round Stingray
UROLOPHUS HALLERI

It is the luckless recreational bather that steps on the Round Stingray—this stinging fish does not actively pursue bathers, but it will sting if stepped on. The stinger is located on the short tail, and can inflict quite a lot of pain. Shuffle your feet along as you move, and it will glide out of your way.

This fish is the most common of stingrays in California waters, and is abundant as far north as Monterey Bay. Unfortunately for beachgoers, stingrays decide to move inshore during summer months, just when humans are moving into the water to cool themselves down. Stingrays will gather in large numbers in hot weather, making for risky bathing.

RANGE: California
ZONE: subtidal to 70 ft
HABITATS: shallows; quiet bays; estuaries; sand and mud
LENGTH: to 22 in
COLOR: brown, gray; mottled yellowish markings

The upper surface of the Round Stingray is light brown or gray, with various mottled markings. These colors help it blend in with the seafloor, where it rests and moves about in search of its favorite foods, such as crabs, shrimps and various snails and clams. The young develop inside the female, and she gives birth to them in quiet bays and estuaries where they remain until they grow and mature.

White-cap Limpet

ACMAEA MITRA

The White-cap Limpet is frequently washed up on shores, where the strong surf pounds the shell to a dull white. Unlike other limpets, with their low profile, the shell of this limpet is very high compared to its length, giving it a pronounced cone-shaped appearance. The base is almost round, and the apex, or high point of the shell, is quite central. The shell is thick and the interior is a smooth white.

When alive, the White-cap Limpet is more likely to appear pink, because it is often coated with Encrusting Coral (p. 199) on which it feeds. Found on exposed, rocky shores, as well as protected, rocky areas, this limpet's high and prominent shell must be a disadvantage in rough surf, but a powerful foot keeps it well adhered to the rock. Look for it at low tide, and do not confuse it with its smaller cousin, the Corded White Limpet (*A. funiculata*), which has ribs radiating from the central apex.

OTHER NAME: Dunce-cap Limpet

RANGE: Southern California to Alaska

ZONE: lower intertidal; subtidal to 100 ft

HABITATS: exposed and protected rocky shores

DIAMETER: to 1.5 in

HEIGHT: to 1 in

COLOR: white shell; with pink growths

Fingered Limpet

LOTTIA DIGITALIS

When you clamber about on the rocks high up on the beach, there are few animals to be noticed. However, the Fingered Limpet, closely hugging rocks, is one of the conspicuous mollusks that you'll find. This limpet's oval shell is colored gray-green and brown, with paler spots flecked here and there. Strong ribs radiate outwards from the apex, the high point, of the shell, making the edge of the shell wavy. The slightly hooked apex is close to the front end of the shell.

This tolerant limpet enjoys the pounding surf, but not the baking sun of the upper intertidal zone. To remain cool, it grazes on algae on vertical surfaces facing the surf and in crevices that offer a bit of protection from the sun. Its powerful foot sucks firmly onto the rock—a great deal of force is needed to remove a limpet, so leave it alone because you risk damaging its shell. Empty limpet shells reveal a glossy white or pale blue interior, with a rich caramel-colored blotch at the apex. A black, wavy margin adds to the limpet's beauty.

OTHER NAMES: Ribbed Limpet; *Collisella digitalis*

RANGE: Southern California to Alaska

ZONE: upper intertidal; spray or splash

HABITATS: exposed, rocky shores

LENGTH: to 1.25 in

COLOR: gray-green, brown; white spots

SIMILAR SPECIES: Rough Limpet (p. 54)

Rough Limpet
LOTTIA SCABRA

The common Rough Limpet closely resembles the Fingered Limpet. It has a variable shell in shades of brown, gray or green. The apex, or high point, of the shell is at the front end, and is not so pronounced, as in the Fingered Limpet. An older Rough Limpet appears to be heavily eroded and pale at the apex. Distinctive ribs radiate from the apex, making a heavily sculptured shell, and the ribs give the shell a scalloped or even saw-toothed margin. The interior of the Rough Limpet is whitish, and has an irregular, brown blob at the apex. Along the scalloped margin is a series of dark spots, not unlike the Fingered Limpet but more coarsely defined.

OTHER NAME: *Collisella scabra*

RANGE: Southern California to Oregon

ZONE: middle to upper intertidal; spray or splash

HABITATS: rocky shores

LENGTH: to 1.25 in

COLOR: variable gray, green and brown

SIMILAR SPECIES: Fingered Limpet (p. 53)

This limpet becomes active at night or when it is submerged by a high tide. Once it has found a favorite location in which to rest, it will return to the same spot again and again. Eventually, by eroding the rock with its tongue, or radula, it leaves a precise scar—'a home scar'—in the rock into which it neatly fits. Such a good fit, however, does little to deter the predatory attentions of the shorebirds and crabs that like to dine on Rough Limpets.

Shield Limpet
LOTTIA PELTA

The Shield Limpet is a small limpet with a heavy shell, usually gray-green in color with white checkers along the outer edge. The color can be variable; young limpets look almost black, while older limpets are worn by the surf and appear chalky. On the inside, a dark caramel center is surrounded by bluish-white, and the shell is bordered with black flecked with paler colors.

In Southern California, most Shield Limpets only grow to a length of 1 inch, while 2 inches is common further north. Look for them in mussel beds and on rocks in the middle to lower intertidal zones, where they feed on red algae, such as Nail Brush (p. 195). Here, these limpets are often challenged by hungry sea stars. When one approaches, the limpet lifts its shell and quickly slithers out of reach.

You might mistake the Shield Limpet for a young Giant Owl Limpet, but the interior of the latter is more richly colored in dark browns. Often found in association with the Shield Limpet is the pale brown File Limpet (*L. limatula*), identified by its fine ribbing, low profile and small, pointed apex at the top of the shell.

OTHER NAMES: *Collisella pelta*
RANGE: Southern California to Alaska
ZONE: middle to lower intertidal
HABITATS: rocky shores; mussel beds; kelp holdfasts
LENGTH: to 1 in
COLOR: gray-green, variable; whitish markings
SIMILAR SPECIES: Giant Owl Limpet (p. 56)

Giant Owl Limpet

LOTTIA GIGANTEA

The largest of the North American limpets gets its name from the dark-colored attachment scar inside its shell, which is said to sometimes resemble the head of an owl. The interior of the shell is highly polished, and can come in shades of brown, blue and white. The shell has been used for making jewelry, because it is often so lovely. The exterior is usually heavily eroded, but white flecks on a generally brown base can be seen along the edge of the shell. The limpet has a very low profile, tucked snugly against the rocks of exposed shores.

RANGE: Southern California to Washington
ZONE: middle intertidal
HABITATS: rocky shores
LENGTH: to 4.5 in
COLOR: brown flecked with white
SIMILAR SPECIES: Shield Limpet (p. 55)

Just like the Rough Limpet, the Giant Owl Limpet etches out a 'home scar,' an eroded depression, that is usually in a clearly defined grazing territory. These depressions are very noticeable when the territory is amongst dense mussel clumps. Look for bare patches of rock that are among the closely packed bivalves. The limpet keeps this area clean and grazes on the algae that colonize the patch. These territories can be very evident in Southern California but become scarcer in the northern limits of this species' range.

Volcano Limpet
FISSURELLA VOLCANO

A number of limpets have holes at their high point, or apex. One of the prettiest is the Volcano Limpet, so named for the crater at its summit and the dark lines of 'lava' flowing down its flanks. Look for this abundant limpet on and under rocks in the middle to lower intertidal zones. This limpet is variably colored in pinks, grays and greens, with darker lines radiating from the apex. The interior is white or faintly green, with a speckled border and a pink line around the hole.

Many Volcano Limpets fall victim to Ochre Sea Stars (p.126). To avoid predators, living limpets will lift up their shells and run as fast as their one big foot is able to carry them.

RANGE: California
ZONE: middle to lower intertidal
HABITATS: rocky shores
LENGTH: to 1.5 in
COLOR: green, reddish, purple, variable; darker lines
SIMILAR SPECIES: Great Keyhole Limpet (p. 58)

The Volcano Limpet has an elongated 'keyhole,' and this keyhole helps to distinguish it from the Rough Keyhole Limpet (*Diadora aspera*) that you might find cast ashore from its subtidal habitat. The Rough Keyhole Limpet has a round keyhole, and is not as glamorously colored. The Great Keyhole Limpet shares the same range, but is quite different in color and form.

Great Keyhole Limpet

MEGATHURA CRENULATA

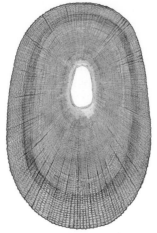

Near the low-tide line lurks one of the largest limpets of all. The shell of the Great Keyhole Limpet can reach the length of 5 inches, and its massive foot can make a living limpet more than 8 inches from head to toe. This large foot cannot be squeezed under the shell. On a living Great Keyhole Limpet, you will notice that the shell is mostly covered by soft gray, brown or black tissue called the 'mantle.' Beneath this mantle is a large and yellow foot on which the limpet moves about while hunting for encrusting growths of various organisms and algae. North of Point Conception, living Great Keyhole Limpets are hard to come by as they retreat into subtidal waters.

RANGE: from Monterey Bay south

ZONE: lower intertidal and subtidal

HABITATS: rocky shores

LENGTH: to 5 in

COLOR: gray or tan shell; whitish interior

SIMILAR SPECIES: Volcano Limpet (p. 57)

A shell denuded of its living resident is usually colored tan or grayish; the interior is white. Coarse to the touch, the surface of the shell is made so by the many tiny ribs radiating from a large and gaping 'keyhole' at the apex of the shell. This hole allows for water currents to circulate around the limpet with ease, keeping it fresh and supplied with oxygen. The Volcano Limpet also has a keyhole, but is very different in color and texture.

Onyx Slipper Shell

CREPIDULA ONYX

In Southern California, the beautiful Onyx Slipper Shell is one of the larger and more conspicuous slipper shells. They can be seen on intertidal rocks and commonly on pilings in bays and harbors. These snails are limpet-like, and are often stuck on other shells. The exterior is a dull brown color, but the interior comes in glossy shades of caramel and brown. The whitish shelf inside is the unusual feature that gives this group of shells their name. At one end of the oval shell is an apex that points off to one side, and from this apex several lines might radiate down the exterior.

RANGE: from Monterey Bay south

ZONE: low-tide line; subtidal to 300 ft

HABITATS: open coasts; bays

LENGTH: to 2 in

COLOR: pale brown exterior; glossy brown interior

These strange mollusks often come in stacks, with older and larger females at the base and smaller males at the top. As they grow, the males will change their sex to female. Slipper shells do not move about like limpets, preferring to stay put and filter the water for tiny nutritious bits and pieces. To find out about the diminutive Slipper Snail (*Crepidula adunca*) refer to the Black Tegula (p. 62).

Spiny Cup-and-Saucer Shell

CRUCIBULUM SPINOSUM

This peculiar shell might be mistaken for a limpet, with its round shell. If you find a yellowish or brown shell covered in tiny spines, however, be sure to check underneath to discover how different it is from the limpets. Underneath, you will discover a white shelf set in a polished brown interior. This shelf is shaped into a funnel or cup, and the two shell parts combined have earned this snail its common name.

RANGE: from Los Angeles south

ZONE: middle to lower intertidal; subtidal to 180 ft

HABITATS: rocky shores; stones; shells

LENGTH: to 2 in

COLOR: white, yellow, brown; white shelf

The shell can grow to 2 inches across, and is often quite elevated, sometimes to as much as 1 inch at the apex. Others can be very flat. Most of the upper surface is covered in spines, although the apex is usually smooth. The white shelf on the interior is placed off to one side. These shells frequently turn up on shore with other dead shells. Live shells can be found attached to stones or other shells in the middle to lower intertidal zones. Here, they remain firmly fixed, gently filtering the water for tiny bits of food.

Black Abalone

HALIOTIS CRACHERODII

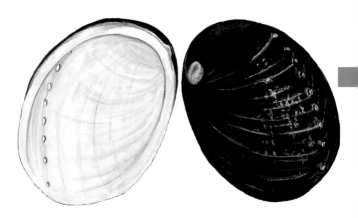

Abalones are prized by people and otters for the firm flesh of the foot. However, the dark-colored foot of this common abalone is a less popular food item than other varieties, such as the larger Red Abalone (*H. rufescens*) that shares the same range. Most often harvested in Southern California is the Pink Abalone (*H. corrugata*), but even the Black Abalone can be hard to find in the intertidal zone because many have been collected; it becomes increasingly rare in Central California. Sucked onto rocks like a limpet, the abalone grazes on a thin film of algae. Please do not remove it out of curiosity—the thin edge of the shell is damaged easily, leaving it vulnerable to predators such as starfish.

RANGE: Southern California to Oregon
ZONE: middle to lower intertidal; subtidal to 20 ft
HABITATS: rocky shores
LENGTH: to 6 in
COLOR: green or blue-black

The Black Abalone's oval shell is blue or greenish-black, and is thicker on one side and smooth in texture. The interior is pearly, and tinted with pinks and greens. The line of holes along the outer edge serves the same purpose as the hole of the Great Keyhole Limpet (p. 58)—it allows a current of water to pass through the shell. Occasionally, the Black Abalone lacks these holes.

61

Black Tegula
TEGULA FUNEBRALIS

Abundant snails of the California coast, Black Tegulas enjoy the harsh upper intertidal reaches of rocky shores along open coasts. Smaller individuals tend to be higher up the shore than the larger individuals, and large aggregations collect in sheltered crevices when the tide is out. These tegulas are herbivores, grazing on the thin film of algae on rocks, as well as on larger pieces of vegetable matter.

OTHER NAME: Black Turban

RANGE: Southern California to Alaska

ZONE: upper to lower intertidal

HABITATS: rocky shores; open coasts

HEIGHT: to 1.75 in

COLOR: black, blue-black

Mostly black or blue-black, the summit of the spire eventually erodes to reveal the shiny pearl surface beneath. Many tegulas will have a hitchhiker or two, including the Black Limpet (*Lottia asmi*) and the Slipper Snail (*Crepidula adunca*), which resembles a limpet. The Black Limpet grazes on algae on the tegula's shell, and will hop onto a new ride when the snails collect together in a group. The Slipper Snail, with its hooked apex, just seems to enjoy the ride, filtering the water from on high. Ochre Sea Stars (p. 126) love to dine on Black Tegulas.

Checkered Periwinkle

LITTORINA SCUTULATA

Several species of periwinkles litter the shores of California, and the Checkered is a likely find. It tolerates the upper intertidal zone, and when the tide retreats it can be found tucked into crevices and among algal holdfasts or mussel beds. A tight-fitting operculum (door) is very important for this creature, because, although it spends so much time exposed to the air, the door, by shutting the snail away inside its shell, makes sure that no moisture is lost. This periwinkle drifts about the rocks grazing on microscopic or larger alga (including the Sea Lettuce, p. 194), and suffers from the hungry attentions of sea stars, especially the Six-rayed Sea Star (p. 129).

RANGE: Southern California to Alaska
ZONE: upper to lower intertidal
HABITATS: rocky shores
LENGTH: to 0.5 in
COLOR: dark brown-black; white checkers

This small periwinkle has a darkly colored shell that is frequently flecked with pale markings, giving a checkered effect. The surface of the shell, unless eroded, is smooth and slightly glossy. You might mistake this periwinkle for the Eroded Periwinkle (*L. keenae*), which usually has brown markings and grows to 0.75 inches in length. The Eroded Periwinkle is so tolerant of the upper intertidal zone that it can be found even higher up than the Checkered Periwinkle, where the surf seldom sprays.

Banded Turban
TEGULA EISENI

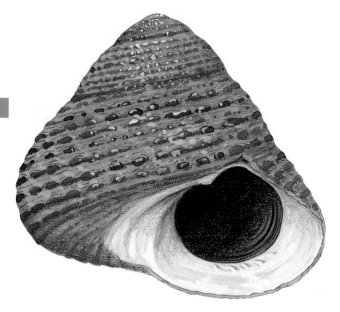

Turbans litter the upper and middle reaches of rocky shores. If they are not filled with a living snail, then they have more than likely become the homes of small hermit crabs. Tidepools can sometimes be filled with twitching turban shells all filled with these crabs. The Banded Turban's brown shell has numerous bands spiraling around the shell, each beaded and sometimes speckled in white or black, resulting in a distinctive appearance and texture. The domed and rounded shell grows to about an inch in height, and is about as wide as it is high.

OTHER NAME: *Tegula ligulata*
RANGE: Southern California
ZONE: middle to lower intertidal
HABITATS: rocky shores
HEIGHT: to 1 in
COLOR: brown

The Speckled Turban Snail (*T. gallina*) shares the same range as the Banded Turban, and it can be more locally abundant north of Los Angeles. This greenish snail is flecked with white markings, giving it a speckled appearance, and it grows a little larger (to 1.5 inches). Both of these turbans withstand long periods out of water. When the tide is out, they close a door on the outside world with a tight-fitting 'operculum,' which seals the moisture in.

Wavy Turban
ASTRAEA UNDOSA

The Wavy Turban is a common and robust shell found at low tide among rocks and kelp. It is easy to identify because of its large size and top-shaped shell. Ridges run vertically as well as spiral around the shell, giving it a wavy appearance. Living examples of the Wavy Turban are often covered in algae and other encrustations. When the snail dies, however, these encrustations are soon worn off. The same thing occurs with the brown periostracum, a fibrous and tough layer on living shells. When the shell is tossed about, this layer is worn away revealing a beautiful pearly layer beneath. Dead shells are frequently washed ashore.

RANGE:	from Point Conception south
ZONE:	lower intertidal; subtidal to 60 ft
HABITATS:	rocky shores; kelp beds
HEIGHT:	to 4 in
COLOR:	light brown

These sturdy shells grow to an impressive 4 inches in height, although the largest are usually confined to kelp beds offshore. Smaller shells can be found near the low-tide line where they will more than likely have shut themselves in with their heavy teardrop-shaped operculum, which keeps predators out and moisture in. In the aperture, or opening, you can catch a glimpse of the pearly layers beneath the brown periostracum.

Lewis's Moonsnail

POLINICES LEWISII

O ne of our largest intertidal snails, the Lewis's Moonsnail can be found burrowing its way in sandy flats. From the aperture a most enormous foot emerges, and is seemingly too much to squeeze back into the shell. The beige foot almost covers the shell, and to tuck it all away, water must be squeezed out through tiny pores. The large, horny operculum (door) then seals it all in.

Lewis's Moonsnail particularly enjoys finding helpless clams stuck and buried in sand. It wraps its foot around them, drills a hole with its radula, and chews out the contents; the empty valves, with the distinctive hole, wash ashore. The Moonsnail does the same thing with the Common Pacific Littleneck (p. 101). In turn, the Moonsnail is pursued by some species of sea stars or occasionally by its own kind. The mystical sand collars of this snail, which wash ashore in summer, are formed around the shell when mucus is secreted. Sand quickly adheres to form a layered sandwich, 6 inches across, and filled with eggs. In southernmost California, the smaller shell (to 3 inches) of the Southern Moonsnail (*Neverita reclusiana*) is also found.

RANGE: Southern California to Alaska

ZONE: lower intertidal; subtidal to 500 ft

HABITATS: sandy flats; bays; quiet waters

HEIGHT: to 5.5 in

COLOR: tan, brown

SIMILAR SPECIES: Norris's Topshell (p. 67)

Norris's Topshell

NORRISIA NORRISII

This large snail is commonly encountered feasting on kelp and other seaweeds near the low-tide line. It is smooth and dark brown, while the foot of the snail is a bright red or orange. This brightly colored foot can make the snail quite obvious when it is crawling about. It is harder to find when it is tucked away inside the shell, shut off from the outside world by its horny, brown 'operculum,' or door.

Norris's Topshell is a rounded shell, rather wider than it is high, and the shell is thick and heavy. Look near the middle of the underside of the shell for a bright green splash of color. Most of the shell is made up of the last big body whorl, which gives it a bulbous appearance similar to Lewis's Moonsnail. The Moonsnail grows larger and is much paler in color. The tiny Turban Slipper Shell (*Crepidula norrisiarum*) is often attached to Norris's Topshell, hitching a permanent ride rather like the slipper shells on the Black Tegula (p. 62). Empty shells are frequently found along the shore.

RANGE: from Point Conception south

ZONE: lower intertidal; subtidal

HABITATS: rocks and seaweed; kelp beds

DIAMETER: to 2.25 in

COLOR: dark brown

SIMILAR SPECIES: Lewis's Moonsnail (p. 66)

Angled Unicorn

ACANTHINA SPIRATA

Angled Unicorns get their mystical name from a prominent spine or horn that sticks out from the lip of the aperture of the shell. Some people speculate that this 'horn' might be used to help tease open the Angled Unicorn's favorite prey of barnacles and bivalves, but actually the snail is armed with a drilling tongue, or radula. With this radula, it drills a small hole through the shell of its prey and then dines on the soft flesh inside. Rocky areas in moderately protected waters are good places to find unicorns. Look among breakwaters and in bays, as well as under rocks in the middle intertidal zone, for groups of them huddled together.

OTHER NAME: Angular Thorn Drupe

RANGE: Southern California to Washington

ZONE: middle intertidal

HABITATS: stones; rocks; mussel beds of moderately protected waters

HEIGHT: to 1.5 in

COLOR: dark gray, yellowish; brown lines

SIMILAR SPECIES: Emarginate Dogwinkle (p. 73)

The Angled Unicorn has pronounced ridges on each whorl of the shell, which produce a tall, stepped spire. The base color is gray or yellowish, and lines revolving around the whorls are usually dark brown. These lines are crossed by pale ribs running the length of the shell, and can result in a checkered appearance. The less common Checkered Unicorn Shell (*A. paucilirata*) is smaller and fatter, and has larger blackish markings, which give it a checkered appearance.

Gem Murex
MAXWELLIA GEMMA

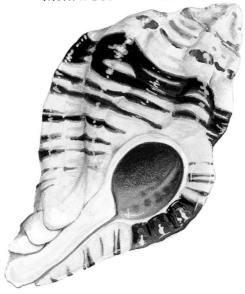

An attractive find on rocky or rubble shores and in breakwaters near the entrance to bays is the Gem Murex. A sturdy shell, it is not quite 2 inches tall. Your best bet for finding a live one is near the low-tide line, but be vigilant for strong surf when the tide starts to come in. It is easy to identify, with its prominent ridges and dark brown stripes that spiral around the white or grayish shell. Some shells can be quite eroded, with worn spires. On less eroded specimens, however, the spire can be beautifully sculptured with deep pits and ridges.

The aperture, or opening, to the shell is very small and almost round. On living specimens, the round opening is tightly filled with an 'operculum,' which is a tough door keeping predators out and, during low tide, moisture in. The operculum is attached to the foot of the snail, and as the snail withdraws into the shell, the operculum neatly follows behind. As the snail grows, so does the operculum to ensure that there is always a snug fit.

RANGE: from Santa Barbara south

ZONE: lower intertidal; subtidal to 180 ft

HABITATS: rocky shores; rubble; breakwaters

HEIGHT: to 1.75 in

COLOR: white, gray; dark bands

Western Mud Whelk

NASSARIUS TEGULUS

Mud flats, while not the most popular places for vacationing or beachcombing, are well worth a visit, especially for the family of mud whelks that reside there. One of the common whelks is the Western Mud Whelk, a small snail with a sharply pointed spire, which only grows to 0.75 inches. What it lacks in size, it often makes up for in color, because this knobby snail can be attractively colored in browns and purples. The 'suture,' or junction between the whorls, is often reddish-brown, and the lip to the aperture is white. Several 'teeth' can be seen inside.

OTHER NAME: Western Mud Nassa

RANGE: from Santa Barbara south

ZONE: lower intertidal

HABITATS: mud flats

HEIGHT: to 0.75 in

COLOR: brown, purple

Mud whelks do a marvelous job at keeping the mud flats clean. At each high tide many dead animals are deposited, along with a coating of microscopic debris called detritus. Mud whelks have an acutely sensitive taste for dead creatures, and within a short time, they will be devouring any corpses. To attract this molluskan garbage collection agency, drop a dead fish on the mud and wait. Study the mud surface to reveal just how many creatures have been crawling across the mud, leaving strange tracks behind.

Joseph's Coat Amphissa
AMPHISSA VERSICOLOR

S mall but strong, Joseph's Coat Amphissa can be a common find near the low-tide line. Tidepools, especially
under rocks and rubble, are a good place to hunt for
this busy little snail. It is an aggressive and carnivorous mollusk, and can be seen moving quickly about the rocks and
among Coralline Algae (p. 198). Closer inspection of the
shell can reveal that a tiny hermit crab has taken up residence. This shell makes an ideal home for a young hermit
crab, until the crab grows and
graduates onto bigger and better shells.

Typically, this amphissa is
yellow or light brown, and is
frequently mottled with pale
and darker markings. Inside the
aperture is a line of small,
rounded 'teeth,' although these
teeth have nothing to do with
biting. The vertical and horizontal ribs result in a gently
beaded texture that is similar to
the texture of the Giant Western Nassa, which grows larger
and more rounded, of mud flats. The Western Lean Nassa
(*Nassarius mendicus*) is similar in size and appearance, though
more highly sculptured, and it prefers sandier habitats.

OTHER NAME: Variegate
Amphissa

RANGE: Southern California
to Washington

ZONE: lower intertidal; subtidal
to 150 ft

HABITATS: rock; rubble; tidepools

HEIGHT: to 0.75 in

COLOR: light brown or yellow;
sometimes mottled

SIMILAR SPECIES: Giant Western
Nassa (p. 72)

Giant Western Nassa

NASSARIUS FOSSATUS

The finely sculptured Giant Western Nassa is a common whelk found in muddy sand where the water is quiet. Growing to 2 inches, it is a large, mostly glossy shell that comes in shades of yellow, brown and gray, with a beaded surface texture. The aperture is wide, and a rich orange colors the inside. The yellowish Western Fat Dogwhelk (*N. perpinguis*) is similar, growing to 1 inch in length and having a more southerly range, only reaching as far north as Central California.

OTHER NAMES: Channeled Dog Whelk; Channeled Basket Shell

RANGE: Southern California to British Columbia

ZONE: middle to lower intertidal; subtidal to 60 ft

HABITATS: sand and mud flats

HEIGHT: to 2 in

COLOR: yellow, brown, gray

SIMILAR SPECIES: Joseph's Coat Amphissa (p. 71)

The Giant Western Nassa prefers the fine sand and mud of bays because it is easier for this robust snail to shuffle its way through the particles. The whelk has a keen nose for decaying matter, and is an active scavenger of the low-tide line, as well as an occasional predator of other shellfish. It is fast moving, which perhaps allows it to get to the food before the many other organisms in this habitat. Don't expect to see Giant Western Nassas racing along the surface of the mud—they are usually buried just below the surface.

Emarginate Dogwinkle

NUCELLA EMARGINATA

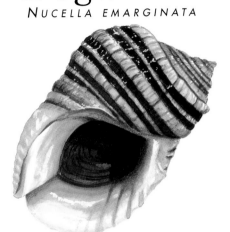

Sometimes shiny, sometimes dull, this highly variable species is a resident of exposed, rocky shores, often in crevices near barnacle and mussel beds. It feeds on both of these creatures, drilling a neat hole in the shell with its serrated tongue, or radula. Of the mussels, it prefers the Blue Mussel (p. 93), perhaps because the shell is thinner and requires less drilling. This dogwinkle also lives on shores that are slightly protected, but is absent from quiet waters.

The stubby shell has a short spire with whitish ribs set against a dark yellow, brown or gray base, which usually results in a striped appearance. The opening to the shell is tinted yellow and a dark brown operculum (door) will be tightly shut against you. The operculum also protects against water loss when the tide is out. Once the snail inside has died, however, hermit crabs enjoy taking up residence in these small and manageable homes. Don't confuse this shell with the Angled Unicorn, which has a taller spire and prominent ridges. The Circled Rockshell (*Ocenebra circumtexta*) is similar in shape, but slightly smaller and with coarser ribs.

| OTHER NAME: Striped Dogwinkle |
| RANGE: Southern California to Alaska |
| ZONE: middle to lower intertidal |
| HABITATS: rocky shores; exposed and semi-protected coasts |
| HEIGHT: to 1 in |
| COLOR: variable, yellow, brown or gray; white stripes |
| SIMILAR SPECIES: Angled Unicorn (p. 68) |

Poulson's Rock Shell
ROPERIA POULSONI

Poulson's Rock Shell is an aggressive carnivore that cruises tidepools of rocky shores and bays in search of mussels and other shelled creatures. Using its drill-like radula, it bores a hole through the shell of the mussel to get at the soft flesh inside. It is itself consumed by some of the larger crabs.

This snail can be easily identified by its tall, gray or white spire, with thin, red lines cutting and spiraling around the shell. Ridges run its length, and these form paler knobs, especially on the large body whorl. A number of 'teeth' can be seen inside the white aperture. This shell will sometimes grow to 2 inches in height, although it is usually smaller.

Kellet's Whelk (*Kellettia kellettii*) shares a similar body shape, and is also striped with reddish or brown lines. However, it grows significantly larger, up to 7 inches, and is a subtidal species so you will only find empty shells that have been cast ashore. The Festive Murex is also similar, but has frills instead of knobs.

OTHER NAME: *Ocenebra poulsoni*
RANGE: from Santa Barbara south
ZONE: middle to lower intertidal; shallow subtidal
HABITATS: rocky shores; bays; pilings
HEIGHT: to 2 in
COLOR: white or gray; red or brown stripes
SIMILAR SPECIES: Festive Murex (p. 75)

Festive Murex
PTEROPURPURA FESTIVA

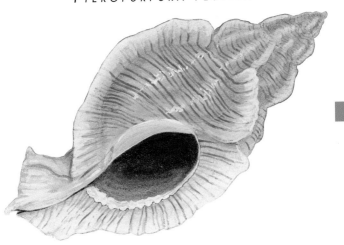

Not many snails enjoy the same diversity of habitats as the Festive Murex does. This lovely shell can be commonly found on mud flats of quiet waters, around rocks in muddy areas and on rocky shores of exposed coasts. The snails on the exposed coasts do not grow as large as those in sheltered areas. Poke about among the seaweeds hanging from pilings—a favorite haunt of the Festive Murex.

Fine brown lines spiral around the yellow-brown shell, and are broken by elegant frills, some of which curl back on themselves. Another distinctive feature of the Festive Murex is the white outer lip of the aperture, which is lined with a series of teeth and appears scalloped. The Nuttall's Hornmouth (*Ceratostoma nuttalli*) shares the frilly features of the Festive Murex, and is also yellow or brownish (and sometimes white). However, it lacks the fine lines and the frills do not curve back on themselves. Compare your find with the Poulson's Rock Shell because they both have thin, reddish-brown lines, although Poulson's Rock Shell has knobs instead of frills.

> OTHER NAMES: Festive Rock Shell; *Shaskyus festiva*
> RANGE: from Santa Barbara south
> ZONE: lower intertidal
> HABITATS: rocks; mud flats; open and protected coasts
> HEIGHT: to 2.75 in
> COLOR: yellow-brown; reddish-brown stripes
> SIMILAR SPECIES: Poulson's Rock Shell (p. 74)

Giant Forreria

FORRERIA BELCHERI

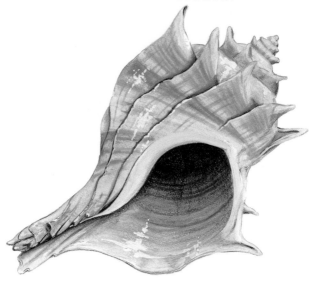

W hile strolling along the sandy beaches of open coasts and bays, you might be lucky to come across the remains of the Giant Forreria. This magnificent shell is one of our largest. Unfortunately, it prefers to live below the low-tide line where it is thought to dine on mussels and oysters. Living examples are seldom found intertidally, and the best encounter we can hope for is when the empty shells wash ashore.

OTHER NAME: Belcher's Murex
RANGE: from Morro Bay south
ZONE: shallow subtidal to 100 ft
HABITATS: sandy coasts; bays; lagoons
HEIGHT: to 6 in
COLOR: yellowish, pale brown

A recently deceased and uneroded specimen will be easy to identify because of its huge size, often as high as 6 inches. If the colors haven't faded, they are a gentle pale yellow or brown with faint darker bands running around the whorls. Numerous frills (usually eight to ten) rise at the shoulders to form large spines. The huge aperture has lips that are white, and a large spine at the shoulder. While the body whorl is large, the spire is short but pointed. Often, the shells that we will find are incomplete, with broken spines, and the colors have faded to a dull white.

Three-winged Murex

PTEROPURPURA TRIALATA

One of the most glamorous finds of the Southern California coastline has to be the Three-winged Murex. This ornate shell comes in shades of brown and cream, often with whitish bands running around the shell. Most characteristic are the three 'wings,' or frills, that have scalloped or fluted edges and can serve as elaborate adornments to the shell. These frills are quite thin and delicate.

You might expect to find such a delicate-looking shell in peaceful waters where its frills will not be damaged. However, this snail prefers rocky coasts, and can often be found on breakwaters at the entrance to bays. Tucked away among the rocks, these snails feast on

OTHER NAME: *Pterynotus trialatus*
RANGE: from Catalina Island south
ZONE: lower intertidal
HABITATS: rocky shores; breakwaters
HEIGHT: to 3 in
COLOR: pale brown, white

other snails. They are especially fond of other mollusks that cannot escape or slide from their grasp, such as the firmly rooted-to-the-spot slipper shells (for example, the Onyx Slipper Shell, p. 59). By drilling through the shell with their sharp 'radula,' or tongue, these snails can reach the soft flesh inside. While searching for these wonderful snails, be sure to keep one eye on the surf, in case the tide is rising.

Tinted Wentletrap
EPITONIUM TINCTUM

Exquisitely sculptured, the Tinted Wentletrap is a tiny treasure. Its unusual name comes from the Danish word for 'spiral staircase,' inspired by the 8 to 14 white ribs running the length of the shell. These ribs are offset against a shell tinted in brown and purple. The round aperture has a thick, white lip, and is closed by a horny operculum when the snail is alive.

OTHER NAME: Painted Wentletrap

RANGE: Southern California to Alaska

ZONE: low-tide line; subtidal to 150 ft

HABITATS: near anemones

HEIGHT: to 0.6 in

COLOR: white; tinted with brown or purple; white ribs

These dainty snails rarely wander far from their food sources—the Aggregating and Giant Green anemones (pp. 141–42). Often buried in sand nearby, Tinted Wentletraps emerge to peck out chunks of the anemone's tentacles and foot. These snails gather in small groups, and when exposed by an ebb tide, burrow and conceal themselves in soft sand. If you notice a wentletrap moving about at speed and in an irregular fashion, you are likely observing the antics of a hermit crab, whose young are rather fond of these shells. A close relative is the lovely Scallop-edged Wentletrap (*E. funiculata*), which lacks the ribs but has a wavy ridge along the junction between the whorls.

Cooper's Turret
HAUSTATOR COOPERI

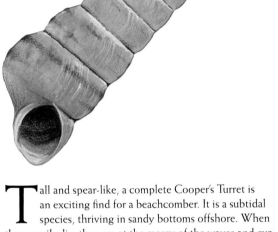

Tall and spear-like, a complete Cooper's Turret is an exciting find for a beachcomber. It is a subtidal species, thriving in sandy bottoms offshore. When these snails die, they are at the mercy of the waves and currents, and shells are frequently washed ashore. By the time they make it into the hands of the beachcomber, the shells are often worn or broken by the sand and waves.

It grows to over 2 inches in height, and the yellowish or tan shell is impressively slender. A mature Cooper's Turret might have as many as 17 whorls. At the base there is a neat circular opening that is usually plugged by a round operculum, a door, that protects the snail when it feels the need to retreat. On some, a pair of ridges runs around and around the shell, giving a slightly rougher texture. These ridges might also be stained with darker colors. In mud flats, creeks, lagoons and marshes, the California Horn Shell (*Cerithidea californica*) is a common find, and resembles Cooper's Turret, except that it is dark brown, more coarsely textured and not so tall (1.75 inches).

OTHER NAME: *Turritella cooperi*
RANGE: from Monterey Bay south
ZONE: subtidal to 300 ft
HABITATS: sandy bottoms offshore
HEIGHT: to 2.25 in
COLOR: tan, yellowish

Ida's Miter
MITRA IDAE

Near the low-tide line along rocky and rubble shores of Southern California, you might be fortunate enough to find the lustrous Ida's Miter. In the northern part of its range, Ida's Miter retreats into deeper subtidal waters. This slender and sharply pointed shell is a member of the Miter family, most of which are found in warm tropical seas. By comparison, this shell is quite a dull example, while the tropical species are large, colorful and often embellished with exquisite markings.

RANGE: California
ZONE: low-tide line; subtidal to 60 ft
HABITATS: rocky and rubble shores
LENGTH: to 3 in
COLOR: black, brown

Ida's Miter is often a glossy black, marked with faint lines revolving around the shell and some vertical lines as well. The black coating is a tough outer layer that covers the shell, and is called a 'periostracum.' On most shells this outer layer wears off, while on a living Ida's Miter it covers most of the shell. Where the coating is eroded, the brown shell is revealed beneath. Dead specimens rapidly lose this black coating when they are tossed and turned by the waves. The long, slender aperture of the shell is whitish, and on the inside three prominent ridges can be seen.

California Cone

CONUS CALIFORNICUS

Small and plain, the California Cone is a dull relative of the exotic and beautifully marked tropical species of cones. The shell is gently rounded and colored in caramels, sometimes with an angled band around the largest whorl of the shell. The short spire and huge main body whorl result in a long and thin aperture out of which the living animal emerges.

This shell is a common find from San Francisco Bay south. To find it, look in gravel and sandy areas and underneath rocks during the day because it is a nocturnal hunter. It has a voracious appetite for many creatures, including other snails. When the California Cone finds a choice prey, it stabs it with a modified tongue, or radula, injects poison that calms the prey, and proceeds to swallow the victim whole. Some tropical species of cone shells are notorious amongst collectors for their potentially dangerous stings, but don't worry about this cone. Along the high-tide line of quiet bays and salt marshes, the Californian Melampus (*Melampus olivaceus*) is a common find that resembles a tiny California Cone.

RANGE: from San Francisco Bay south

ZONE: low-tide line; subtidal to 100 ft

HABITATS: mixed rock; gravel and sandy areas

LENGTH: to 1.5 in

COLOR: pale brown

Large Coffee Bean

TRIVIA SOLANDRI

This attractive snail can be found in the southernmost counties of California. In shape it resembles and is related to the tropical and colorful cowries. The Large Coffee Bean is purplish-brown in color (hence its common name), and has a pale stripe down the middle of the back. The upper side is rounded, while the underside is flat. Pale ribs curve around from the upper side to the lower, giving a toothed margin to the shell's long, thin aperture.

RANGE: from Catalina Island south

ZONE: low-tide line; subtidal to 250 ft

HABITATS: rocks; seaweeds; tunicates

LENGTH: to 0.5 in

COLOR: purplish-brown; whitish ribs

When living and active, the soft, fleshy mantle of the mollusk emerges and wraps over most of the upper surface of the shell, rather like an elaborate overcoat.

Trivias, such as the Large Coffee Bean, feed on tunicates and other soft organisms. Thus, they will usually be found near their favorite food source, as well as among rocks and seaweeds near the low-tide line and in subtidal waters. The common Small Coffee Bean (*T. californiana*) is, as its name implies, smaller, and can be found further north. This shell lacks the Large Coffee Bean's white beads that form at the ends of the ribs and are next to the pale stripe.

Chestnut Cowry
CYPRAEA SPADICEA

Southern California can boast about having the only cowry in the West, even if it is rare north of Santa Barbara. The cowries are a large family of shells, nearly all of which are beautifully colored and tropical. With their glamorous looks and polished surfaces, collectors prize them, which possibly makes Chestnut Cowries scarcer today than they otherwise would be. Please reserve your collection to the dead and empty shells washed ashore!

The lovely Chestnut Cowry is whitish on the underside, where there is a long, slender aperture lined with small teeth. On top there are blobs of caramel, chestnut and tan colors that richly glow under the bright polish of the shell. When this mollusk is active, its soft, orange mantle rises up and over the shell, keeping it clean and shiny by leaving new shell deposits on the surface. A good-sized Chestnut Cowry will be 2.5 inches in length, although larger shells are known. The cowry creeps about on a white foot, consuming soft-bodied animals like anemones and tunicates.

OTHER NAME: *Zonaria spadicea*
RANGE: from Monterey Bay south
ZONE: lower intertidal; subtidal to 120 ft
HABITATS: rocks; stones; under protected ledges; kelp beds
LENGTH: to 2.5 in
COLOR: white, tan, brown

The 0.5-inch Appleseed Erato (*Erato vitellina*) is like a miniature version of the Chestnut Cowry. The Appleseed Erato is purplish and is found as far north as Bodega Bay.

Purple Dwarf Olive

OLIVELLA BIPLICATA

A celebrated find among beachcombers, the Purple Dwarf Olive has a highly polished shell with variable and beautiful colors. This snail is elongated and tapered at both ends, rather resembling a slippery olive fruit. Its pointed ends and smooth surface help it burrow through the sand, while its large foot propels it along. By day this snail is concealed well below the surface, with perhaps just a slight dimple in the sand hinting at its presence. At night it moves to the surface, with the top of its shell often poking through.

Gray and purple are the dominant colors of the Purple Dwarf Olive, with brown stripes marking the suture of the short spire. The aperture is long, allowing the extensive foot to come out. A long siphon is used to suck water down from the surface.

RANGE: Southern California to Alaska

ZONE: middle to lower intertidal; subtidal to 150 ft

HABITATS: sandy beaches and flats

LENGTH: to 1.25 in

COLOR: variable purple, brown, gray

Purple Dwarf Olives gather in groups, perhaps as foraging parties, which certainly makes finding a mate easier in the vast expanses of sand. They sift the sand for decaying bits and pieces of organic material and occasionally take small prey. In turn these snails are the victims of the other common sand resident, the Lewis's Moonsnail (p. 66).

Striped Barrel Snail

RICTAXIS PUNCTOCAELATUS

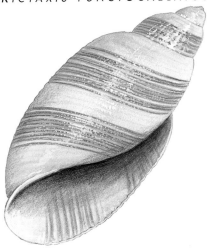

This delicate snail is a locally abundant resident of sand flats and mud flats on protected coasts of Southern California. Further north, it is confined to deeper waters, which makes it harder to come by. Occasionally gathering in large numbers, it feeds on tiny deposits left on the surface of the sand and mud. Striped Barrel Snails also turn up in sandy tidepools and between the roots of eelgrass plants.

The shell is delicate and appears bulbous, hence its delightful other name of 'Carpenter's Baby Bubble.' The whitish shell is small, less than 1 inch in length, and it is adorned with two broad bands of bluish-gray. On closer inspection, you will notice that these bands are each a collection of parallel lines. With the bubbly shape comes a very large aperture, or opening, to the shell. Through this aperture, the snail can squeeze its large, white foot up into the shell. Some snails possess an operculum, much like a door, with which they seal themselves in; the Striped Barrel Snail does not.

OTHER NAME: Carpenter's Baby Bubble

RANGE: Southern California to Alaska

ZONE: lower intertidal; subtidal to 300 ft

HABITATS: sand flats; tidepools; eelgrass beds; protected coasts

LENGTH: to 0.75 in

COLOR: white; dark bands

California Paper Bubble

BULLA GOULDIANA

Southern California is blessed with many beautiful shells, and the California Paper Bubble is one that is confined to this region of the West Coast. This snail is appropriately named, with its thin, almost papery shell and large, bulbous body whorl. The California Paper Bubble peruses the mud flats of estuaries, lagoons and quiet-water bays at low tide. It can only be found south of Santa Barbara, and some of its habitats are being lost to development by shore-hungry humans.

The thin shell is gray-brown and flecked with darker markings that have a white band on the aperture side. The shell is so thin that the markings on the outside show through to the inside. Living snails have a huge 'mantle,' a flap of soft tissue that rises up and over the shell, often covering it. When prodded by a curious beachcomber, the snail quickly retreats into its shell, but its foot is so huge it is impossible for it to squeeze all the way in.

If you find a similar, but really small whitish shell in the same habitats, it is probably the White Bubble Snail (*Haminoea vesicula*).

OTHER NAME: Cloudy Paper Bubble

RANGE: from Santa Barbara south

ZONE: lower intertidal; subtidal to 150 ft

HABITATS: mud flats; very quiet bays

LENGTH: to 2 in

COLOR: gray-brown; dark brown markings

Speckled Scallop

ARGOPECTEN AEQUISULCATUS

Scallop-eaters would love to get their hands on this tasty morsel, and it was once so avidly collected that its numbers fell into sharp decline. Luckily for the Speckled Scallop, state law now prohibits its collection.

The Speckled Scallop can be found at the low-tide line of sand flats in quiet bays and estuaries. The round shell is bright orange or red, with darker red or purplish markings. There are about 20 rounded ribs that give the scallop its distinctive scalloped edge. The interior of the shell is whitish, with some darker markings. Living scallops have a line of well-developed eyes between the two shells. With their strong vision, they watch for approaching intruders. It is hard to believe, but these bivalves are competent swimmers; they will start into a flapping frenzy, swimming away from hungry sea stars or beachcombers by propelling water from their shells.

RANGE: from Santa Barbara south

ZONE: low-tide line; subtidal to 150 ft

HABITATS: sand flats; bays; estuaries

DIAMETER: to 3.5 in

COLOR: bright orange or red; dark reddish or purplish markings

SIMILAR SPECIES: juvenile Giant Rock Scallop (p. 88)

Lucky beachcombers might come across the huge shell of a San Diego Scallop (*Pecten diegensis*) that has been cast ashore. This scallop, which has a diameter of 5 inches, lives in the deeper waters of Southern California.

Giant Rock Scallop

CRASSODOMA GIGANTEUS

So tasty is this prized delicacy that it's a lucky naturalist who finds one intertidally. This slow-growing scallop lives up to 50 years, so think about the life you are removing before you harvest one.

As a juvenile, the Giant Rock Scallop is free-swimming, and it might be confused with the Speckled Scallop. Fairly soon, though, this scallop settles on a rock and sticks to it. Thereafter, the upper valve grows irregularly with the rock and becomes encrusted with sponges, worms and anything else that mistakes the scallop for a rock. It can take about 25 years for a Giant Rock Scallop to become full grown, and quite a size it can reach, too.

If this scallop is observed alive, the flesh on the gaping shell is a brilliant orange, and its small, blue eyes line the gap. Empty upper valves frequently turn up on the shore in fragments, but they are still easily identified by a deep purple stain in the hinge area. Native peoples once used the shells for jewelry and ground up the burnt shells to make paints. No doubt, they didn't let the colorful flesh go to waste either.

OTHER NAMES: Purple-hinged Rock Scallop; *Hinnites giganteus*

RANGE: Southern California to Alaska

ZONE: lower intertidal; subtidal to 150 ft

HABITATS: rocky shores

LENGTH: to 10 in

COLOR: juveniles are orange; adults are encrusted with other organisms

SIMILAR SPECIES: Speckled Scallop (p. 87) resembles a juvenile Giant Rock Scallop

Clear Jewel Box
CHAMA ARCANA

The upper valve of the Clear Jewel Box is frequently washed up on shore. It is easily recognizable by the unusual leafy appendages adorning its outer surface, and it is tough enough to withstand the beating of the surf. The shell is mostly white both inside and out, but the outside is often tinged with pink or orange, especially near the umbo. This mollusk's common name reflects the shell's translucent quality.

The left or lower valve of the Clear Jewel Shell will seldom be found cast up on the shore. The lower valve is very thick and deeply dished, and it remains securely fastened to the rocks near the low-tide line or in subtidal waters.

This jewel box is often found on and under rocks, and although it can occur as far north as Oregon, it is seldom found north of San Francisco Bay. Another jewel box that shares the same range is the Reversed Jewel Box or Chama (*Pseudochama exogyra*), which attaches to rocks with its right valve and is rarely colored as beautifully as the Clear Jewel Box.

OTHER NAME: Agate Chama

RANGE: Southern California to Oregon

ZONE: middle to lower intertidal; subtidal to 260 ft

HABITATS: rocky shores; gravel

LENGTH: to 3.5 in

COLOR: translucent white; pink or orange tint

False Pacific Jingle Shell

PODODESMUS CEPIO

These shells are said to jingle when rolling in the surf. They are distinctive shells that are commonly found on hard substrates, such as rocks and other shells. When a young jingle shell settles onto a suitable rock, it sends strong filaments, or byssal threads, through the hole in the lower valve to attach it to the rock. The shell then grows into the shape of the rock to which it is attached. The whitish upper valve is complete and roughly circular. The interior is glossy. Algae growing in the shell can give the outside a greenish tinge.

OTHER NAMES: Abalone Jingle; Rock Oyster; Green False-Jingle

RANGE: Southern California to Alaska

ZONE: intertidal; subtidal to 300 ft

HABITATS: rocky shores

LENGTH: to 4 in

COLOR: whitish interior; greenish exterior

On the above illustration, look for the large, round muscle scar on the upper valve's interior. Put the two valves together, and the scar lines up with the hole in the lower valve. It is a strong muscle that keeps these shells attached to the rocks.

Two forms of the False Pacific Jingle Shell occur in California: north of Monterey Bay, the shell is thicker and more coarsely ribbed on the upper surface (and might go by the name of *P. macrochisma macrochisma*); south of Monterey Bay and throughout Southern California, the shell is thin and delicately marked (sometimes called *P. m. cepio*).

Native Pacific Oyster
OSTREA LURIDA

The Native Pacific Oyster is found in many intertidal habitats, such as mud flats, gravel banks, tidepools, estuaries, rocks, pilings and other shells. The valves grow rather irregularly, being shaped by the substrate onto which they are attached, and no two shells will look the same. The exterior is a cream to gray, with white or darker markings, and there are visible but irregular growth rings. The interior is smooth and white, with green or blue tints.

These oysters are rather indecisive about their sex, and they will switch from being female one year to male the next.

The Native Pacific Oyster was once abundant along much of the West Coast, but it has suffered from the toxic effects of pulp mill effluents in many regions. Attempts have been made to reintroduce this oyster to the worst effected areas, such as in some Oregon estuaries. North of Point Conception, another oyster is commonly found. This species is the Giant Pacific Oyster (*Crassotrea gigas*), which really is a giant, growing to as much as 12 inches. The Native Pacific Oyster only grows to 3.5 inches, but many consider it to have a superior taste.

OTHER NAME: Olympia Oyster

RANGE: Southern California to Alaska

ZONE: low-tide line; subtidal to 165 ft

HABITATS: flats; tidepools; estuaries; firm substrates

LENGTH: to 3.5 in

COLOR: cream and gray; heavily marked

California Mussel
MYTILUS CALIFORNIANUS

Large and unmistakable, this mussel thrives in the pounding surf of open coasts. Strong, protein-rich byssal threads extend from the foot of the mussel and cling tenaciously to a rock or to other mussels. Huge 'beds' of mussels frequently form in bands along the rocky shores. One atop another, the unfortunate individuals at the bottom might have a hard time holding onto the rock, and large waves can tear out chunks of the bed. New colonies will soon form on the newly exposed rock.

RANGE: Southern California to Alaska

ZONE: middle to lower intertidal; subtidal to 330 ft

HABITATS: rocks; pilings; exposed coasts

LENGTH: to 8 in; larger subtidally

COLOR: blue-black and brown

SIMILAR SPECIES: Blue Mussel (p. 93)

The thick, gorgeous shells of this mussel are usually blue, with hints of brown. The tough, bluish periostracum can be seen peeling off dead shells. Low-profile ribs radiate out from the hinge of the shell. The interior surface is glossy blue and white, and a few small but worthless pearls can sometimes be found. In quieter bays, another large mussel, the Fat Horse Mussel (*Modiolus capax*), can be found. This mussel is brown with a hairy coating on parts of the shell.

If mussels are a favorite food for you, be warned that summer harvesting can be dangerous because the orange flesh accumulates paralytic poisons from the notorious 'red tide.'

Blue Mussel
MYTILUS EDULIS

Smaller than the California Mussel and less hardy, this delicate mussel is found in protected waters, often where there is low salinity (when fresh water mixes with seawater). Under the right conditions, the two mussels can be seen growing together. The Blue Mussel lacks the ribs and uneven texture of the California Mussel. While brown shells are quite common in the Blue Mussel, most of the long, elegant shells are blue-black. The interior of their valves is blue-white. The Ribbed Mussel (*Ischadium demissum*) can sometimes be seen alongside. It is about the same size, but it has fine ribs down its length.

Attached to rocks and wood, especially pilings, the Blue Mussel can form dense mats that are excellent habitats for many other organisms, which enjoy shelter and protection between the shells. As the gentle waves fall over them, the mussels take water into their shells, where they filter out tiny particles of food. The Blue Mussel's small size deters many human hunters, and it avoids the predatory whelks of the open coast by living in quiet waters, but these thin-shelled bivalves are a favorite food of crabs, birds and starfish.

OTHER NAMES: Edible Mussel; Bay Mussel; *M. trossulus*

RANGE: Southern California to Alaska

ZONE: middle to lower intertidal; subtidal to 16 ft

HABITATS: quiet waters; rocks; wood pilings

LENGTH: to 4 in

COLOR: blue-black and brown

SIMILAR SPECIES: California Mussel (p. 92)

California Jack-knife Clam

TAGELUS CALIFORNIANUS

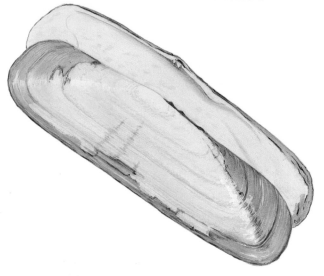

Beneath the surface of muddy and sandy flats, many jack-knife clams often lurk. They dig burrows to depths of about 20 inches in the fine sediment. When they feed, they come close to the surface to filter the water. An approaching angler, however, will be enough to scare these clams to the bottom of their burrow for protection—they are a favorite bait for anglers.

OTHER NAME: California Tagelus
RANGE: California
ZONE: intertidal
HABITATS: sand and mud flats
LENGTH: to 4.25 in
COLOR: whitish and yellow; brown coating

Although this clam is found north to Humboldt Bay, it is not common north of Santa Barbara. The California Jack-knife Clam, the most abundant of its kind in Southern California, can be distinguished by the position of its hinge close to the middle of the shell. Mostly whitish or yellow, parts of the shell are covered in a brown, fibrous layer that is often worn away. On some shells there are thin, reddish lines near the hinge.

A slightly smaller clam that is not so common is the Rosy Razor Clam (*Solen rosaceus*). This pinkish clam has a hinge near one end of the shell.

Bean Clam
DONAX GOULDI

A stroll along a wave-washed sandy beach is made complete by the discovery of Bean Clam shells. Although small, these attractive shells are a treat to collect because they come in a variety of colors, from white to yellow, brown, blue or many more. The exterior is sometimes banded as well. The interior of the shell is stained with a rich purple, and both inside and out are smooth to the touch and glossy.

Bean Clams are almost triangular, with one end extended and rounded. Clams that have recently died still have both valves attached, but after a short period of thrashing by the waves, the shells separate and are found singly. The living clams favor sandy beaches and are buried just below the surface. For reasons unknown, these clams have population explosions. Some years they are so abundant that the beaches are carpeted with their shells, while in other years they almost disappear. The Bean Clam prefers open coasts where the surf is strong. In calmer waters, the similar Wedge Clam (*D. californicus*) can be found. This clam grows slightly larger but is not as colorful.

RANGE: from Santa Barbara south

ZONE: intertidal

HABITATS: sandy, wave-washed beaches

LENGTH: to 1 in

COLOR: very variable; purplish interior

Common Pacific Egg

LAEVICARDIUM SUBSTRIATUM

These small shells are abundant in quiet waters, such as bays and estuaries, from Catalina Island south. They bury themselves in the soft sand near the low-tide line. The shells are typically oval, inflated and mostly smooth. The exterior is tan or yellowish, sometimes with darker streaking. Close inspection will reveal many tiny ribs, especially around the outer edge. The interior is yellowish as well, but is for the most part stained with darker reddish-browns. The smooth inner surface makes for a glossy and attractive finish. Numerous tiny, comb-like teeth line the inner edge of the shell, but the edge remains quite smooth.

The Common Pacific Egg belongs in the Cockle family, of which there are many species in the seas of the world. When viewed from the side, a complete cockle has a heart-shaped appearance, earning it the name of 'heart clam.' A roundish shell with which the Common Pacific Egg might be confused is the Common Pacific Littleneck. This bivalve grows larger and has growth rings and ribs that give it a rougher texture.

OTHER NAME: Little Egg Cockle

RANGE: from Catalina Island south

ZONE: lower intertidal; subtidal to 150 ft

HABITATS: quiet waters; bays; estuaries; sand flats

DIAMETER: to 1.25 in

COLOR: tan or yellow; interior has brown markings

SIMILAR SPECIES: Common Pacific Littleneck (p. 101)

Bent-nosed Macoma

MACOMA NASUTA

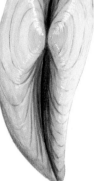

The thin, white shells of the Bent-nosed Macoma have the unique habit of bending to one side. This habit is explained by the bivalve's preference for lying on its side and sending its siphons to the surface. Buried just 4 to 6 inches under the surface, the orange siphons extend upwards to sift for tasty sediments on the muddy sands. Once the clam has vacuumed up every morsel, it digs its way along to new territory and starts again.

The Bent-nosed Macoma is common in bays and quieter waters along the open coast. Being only a few inches below the surface, it often falls victim to the dreaded Lewis's Moonsnail (p. 66). Clams that have been preyed on by this snail bear a distinctive drilled hole through the shell. These dead shells frequently wash up on the shore; empty shells are plain white inside, much the same as the worn exterior.

| OTHER NAME: Bent-nosed Clam |
| RANGE: Southern California to Alaska |
| ZONE: intertidal; subtidal to 150 ft |
| HABITATS: muddy sands of open bays; open coasts |
| LENGTH: to 3 in |
| COLOR: mostly white |
| SIMILAR SPECIES: California Mactra (p. 98); Pismo Clam (p. 99) |

The White Sand Macoma (*M. secta*) resembles the Bent-nosed Macoma, but lacks the distinctive bend and grows to over 4 inches in length.

California Mactra

MACTROTOMA CALIFORNICA

One of the more common surf clams to be found cast ashore is the California Mactra. This unelaborate clam is white, and is partially covered with a thin, brownish-gray periostracum. When the periostracum is worn away, as is often the case with shells that have been battered by waves for some time, the shell is all white. The small clam shell is quite thin and smooth, and the interior is also white.

The California Mactra lives buried in sand or muddy sand, most often in quiet waters. Where it is locally abundant, it is gathered for the ever-popular clam chowder. Further north, in Central California, this clam becomes scarce, and clam-hungry humans must direct their attentions elsewhere.

There are many surf clams, mactras, macomas and similar bivalves that are cast ashore on sandy beaches after storms, and identifying them can present some challenges. Be sure to double check your find with the other bivalves in this section of the book, such as the Pismo Clam and the Bent-nosed Macoma.

OTHER NAMES: California Surf Clam; *Mactra californica*

RANGE: Southern and Central California

ZONE: intertidal; subtidal to 70 ft

HABITATS: sand; muddy sand; bays

LENGTH: to 2 in

COLOR: white and gray-brown

SIMILAR SPECIES: Bent-nosed Macoma (p. 97); Pismo Clam (p. 99)

Pismo Clam

TIVELA STULTORUM

So many abundant creatures of the West Coast have been at the mercy of human consumption, and the hefty Pismo Clam is yet another one of them. This clam was even harvested to feed to livestock. Over-harvesting of it led to such a serious decline in populations that there are now laws to limit its collection. Be sure to check the current regulations before taking any.

The Pismo Clam, an impressively large clam, is up to 7 inches long and has the shape of a rounded triangle. The buff or gray shell is polished smooth and often marked with darker rays. The interior is whitish. The living bivalve lives just below the surface of the sand in quiet waters. The short siphons, with which it sucks in water to filter for food, keep it

RANGE: Southern and Central California

ZONE: low-tide line; shallow subtidal

HABITATS: sandy shores; semi-protected coasts

LENGTH: to 7 in

COLOR: buff or gray; darker rays

SIMILAR SPECIES: Sunset Clam (p. 100); Bent-nosed Macoma (p. 97); California Mactra (p. 98)

close to the surface and make it an easy target for all kinds of predators aside from humans. Sea Otters (p. 31) adore this clam, so remember, when you are next tempted to harvest Pismo Clams, you might well be depriving many other creatures of a much-needed meal!

Sunset Clam
GARI CALIFORNICA

The Sunset Clam has earned its name from the pinkish rays on the outer surface of the shells—the kind of rays you would hope to see in a perfect sunset. The outer surface of the shell is mostly cream-colored; it is pure white on the inside. Small bits and pieces of the brown outer coating, or periostracum, might be left around the edge of the shell. This large bivalve is smooth to the touch. Empty shells frequently turn up near sand or gravel areas of rocky shores, as well as in quiet waters, such as estuaries and bays.

RANGE: Southern California to Alaska

ZONE: low-tide line; subtidal to 150 ft

HABITATS: gravel; sand; between rocks; sand flats in quiet waters

LENGTH: to 4 in

COLOR: cream; pinkish rays

SIMILAR SPECIES: Pismo Clam (p. 99)

The living clam remains buried in the sand or gravel, connected to the surface by its fleshy siphons. The longer siphon inhales water, while the short siphon exhales it, creating a flow of seawater down into the clam. The water flow serves two main purposes: the clam filters the water for small pieces of food, and the fresh water provides oxygen. The exhaled water carries with it the clam's waste products.

Common Pacific Littleneck

PROTOTHACA STAMINEA

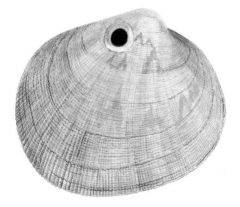

A poor digger, this littleneck can be found in abundance in firm, muddy gravel. It has short siphons, for which it gets the 'littleneck' name, that keep it close to the surface, making harvesting easy for enthusiasts hungry for some cockle flesh. Unfortunately for this bivalve, the small jets of seawater it produces easily mark its location. If you are set on eating littlenecks, show some respect for the other organisms by using a small tool to extract your target. The minimum size harvestable is 1.5 inches, which ensures that the clam will not be over-harvested.

The finely textured surface of the shell results from the many radiating and concentric ridges formed by the ribs and growth lines. Usually whitish in color, there can be tints of yellow, and darker brown markings often take the form of zigzags. The shell is quite thick, but not thick enough to deter the predatory Lewis's Moonsnail (p. 66) from drilling a hole near the hinge and consuming the littleneck. Moonsnail victims wash up on the shore, so be sure to look for the telltale hole.

OTHER NAMES: Native Littleneck; Rock Cockle; Steamer Clam

RANGE: Southern California to Alaska

ZONE: middle to lower intertidal; shallow subtidal

HABITATS: coarse sand; mud; gravel; quieter waters

LENGTH: to 3 in

COLOR: tinted white; brown markings

SIMILAR SPECIES: Common Pacific Egg (p. 96)

101

Common Washington Clam

SAXIDOMUS NUTTALLI

The Common Washington Clam is a rounded clam with prominent concentric ridges. The large, oval shell is usually grayish on the outside and white inside. The outer surfaces are occasionally flecked with darker markings that are stains from iron sulfides (chemical compounds found in low-oxygen environments, such as the deep mud and sand where this clam likes to live). Bays and offshore waters far from the rough surf are preferred by the Common Washington Clam. Large clams can be as much as 20 years old, and often host tiny pea crabs (*Pinnixa* spp.) inside their shells.

OTHER NAME: Butter Clam

RANGE: Southern and Central California

ZONE: low-tide line; subtidal to 150 ft

HABITATS: mud; sand; bays; offshore

LENGTH: to 4.75 in

COLOR: grayish

SIMILAR SPECIES: Wavy Chione (p. 103)

This clam's range in California overlaps with its close relative, the Smooth Washington Clam (S. *gigantea*), which, as its name implies, is smoother, lacking the prominent ridges. The Smooth Washington Clam occupies the mud of Central California and further north, while the Common Washington Clam is found in the mud and sand of southern and central regions of the state (although it is scarcer in Southern California). Both are important contributors to the clam industry. Regulations sensibly restrict the harvesting of these shellfish, ensuring that there will be clams for many years to come.

Wavy Chione

CHIONE UNDATELLA

There are several species of chione to be found in Southern California. The most commonly encountered species is the Wavy Chione, which is often cast up empty on the shore. This bivalve is white or grayish, and frequently colored with brown chevrons and other markings. Old beach-worn shells are white from the sun and abrasive sand. The most distinguishing features on the shell are the prominent, concentric, wavy frills and the ridges that radiate from the hinge. Look for these ornate clams along sandy beaches, bays and lagoons. Dead shells might have a distinctive hole drilled near the hinge, a sure sign that the bivalve was a victim of the predatory Lewis's Moonsnail (p. 66).

Another chione you might encounter is the California Chione (*C. californiensis*), which has fewer frills that are more widely spaced. It can be locally more common than the Wavy Chione. The Smooth Chione (*C. fluctifraga*) retains the shape of the Wavy Chione but lacks any prominent ribs and ridges, resulting in a smooth surface. Of the three, it is the Wavy Chione that is most often harvested for culinary purposes.

OTHER NAME: Frilled California Venus

RANGE: from Santa Barbara south

ZONE: intertidal; subtidal to 30 ft

HABITATS: sandy beaches; bays; lagoons; creeks

LENGTH: to 2 in

COLOR: white or gray; brown markings

SIMILAR SPECIES: Common Washington Clam (p. 102)

Pacific Gaper

TRESUS NUTTALLII

This clam is one of the largest in California, weighing as much as 4 pounds. The lengthy siphons are so voluminous that it cannot withdraw them into the two valves. Thus, when dug up, the Pacific Gaper is most definitely gaping. If you are plodding about on sand or mud flats in quiet waters, the clam retracts its fused siphons and shoots a jet of water into the air. Jump up and down, and you can really get them going! The flesh of harvested Pacific Gapers is popular among some shellfish aficionados, some of whom can be observed digging to great depths to obtain these chunky meals. Unfortunately for Pacific Gapers, the squirting water is a dead giveaway to their exact locations.

This white or yellowish clam is tucked as much as 3 feet under the surface and has a brown coating where the periostracum has not worn away. Few other shellfish can survive at such depths under the surface of the sand or mud, but the Pacific Gaper has much longer siphons than most clams.

OTHER NAMES: Summer Clam; Otter Clam; Horseneck Clam

RANGE: Southern California to Alaska

ZONE: low intertidal; subtidal to 100 ft

HABITATS: sand flats; mud flats; protected beaches; estuaries

LENGTH: to 9 in

COLOR: white or yellowish; brown coating

Nuttall's Cockle
CLINOCARDIUM NUTTALLI

This shell is a delight to find, and if both valves are still joined at the hinge, they make a beautiful heart-shape when viewed from the ends. Strongly ribbed, the grayish shell is covered in a rich yellow to brown periostracum. The interior of the almost circular valves is a pale yellow-white. Well-defined ribs give a scalloped edge to the shell, and darker growth rings are evident. Much older Nuttall's Cockles have noticeably worn ribs. Younger cockles might show some darker mottling on the shell.

The short siphons restrict the cockle from burrowing too deeply, and it often sits on or near the surface of muddy sands. To cope with this high-risk environment, the cockle has a muscular foot. When a hungry sea star gets too close, the cockle can flip and jump about, evading the star's grasping arms. Such strategies allow the cockle to live for up to 16 years. It is less adept, however, at escaping commercial fishing—this cockle is a favorite for many people.

OTHER NAMES: Basket Cockle; Heart Cockle

RANGE: Southern California to Alaska

ZONE: low intertidal; subtidal to 180 ft

HABITATS: mud; sand; gravel; quiet waters

LENGTH: to 5.5 in

COLOR: gray; brown to yellow-brown coating

Little Heart Clam

GLANS SUBQUADRATA

Attached to the underside of rocks and occasionally on pilings, you might come across the coarsely ribbed Little Heart Clam. Check under rocks at low tide. Like a mussel, this little bivalve attaches itself to rocks with byssal threads. The oblong shell has about 15 rounded ribs that have a knobby texture. These ribs give the shell a very distinct scalloped edge. The shell is tan-colored, and covered with a thin, brown periostracum, a tough outer coating that covers the shell. The inside of the shell is pale purplish.

This solid little clam has deep inflated shells. The Little Heart Clam has the unusual habit of keeping its eggs and young inside these two valves, in a similar fashion to a mother kangaroo looking after her baby in a pouch. Most bivalves release their eggs liberally into the water. A relative of the Little Heart Clam—the Stout Heart Shell (*Americardia biangulata*)—frequently turns up on shores near where there has been some disturbance, such as dredging. This shell is slightly larger (over 1 inch long), and a dead shell is usually white once it has lost its brown periostracum.

OTHER NAMES: Carpenter's Cardita; *Glans carpenteri*

RANGE: Southern California to British Columbia

ZONE: middle to lower intertidal; subtidal to 300 ft

HABITATS: rocks; pilings

LENGTH: to 0.5 in

COLOR: tan, brown

Pacific Shipworm

BANKIA SETACEA

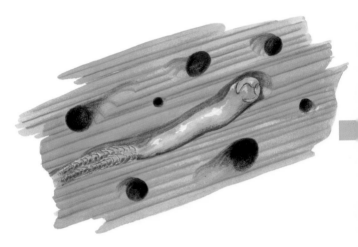

Feared by the wooden shipbuilders of the past, the Pacific Shipworm can destroy wooden structures with its burrowing antics. Not a worm at all, but a greatly extended bivalve, the shipworm has two sharply serrated shells that it uses to carve a home in the wood. These tiny shells are white, and the burrows are lined with a calcareous secretion. At the rear end are two odd feathery structures called 'pallets.' These tiered ornaments protect two siphons that pump water in and out of the burrow, and plug the entrance.

Young shipworms are free-swimming, soon settling on wood. It is easier for them to burrow along the grain of the wood, and although a plank might be riddled with burrows, they never cross over each other. Digesting some of the wood, shipworms rely more on filtering the seawater through the burrow entrance, and extracting the planktonic wildlife. Break open some driftwood to expose the mollusks within. If they have long since died, their shells and pallets might still be inside. Near shore, the burrowing antics are more likely to be from the much smaller shipworm, *Lyrodus pedicellatus*.

OTHER NAME: Feathery Shipworm

RANGE: Southern California to Alaska

ZONE: intertidal and offshore

HABITATS: wood only

LENGTH: shell 0.25 in; body to 3.3 ft

COLOR: white shell

Merten's Chiton
LEPIDOZONA MERTENSII

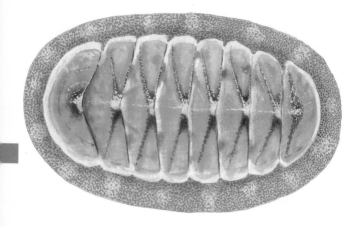

A little bit of searching is required to find these little ocean gems. Merten's Chiton is most often stuck to the underside of rocks in the intertidal zone, but it also lives in deeper water. When turning rocks in the hunt for this mollusk, replace them very carefully; don't damage the chiton and the wealth of other creatures living there. A chiton is never in a hurry, and it can hang out in the same spot for many years—reportedly for as long as 25 years in some cases! Such persistent grazing on the same rock might result in an eroded depression underneath the chiton.

Merten's Chiton is intricately marked and has a girdle surrounding the plates. The girdle, which is made from tiny scales in this chiton, is reddish-brown with paler patches that can appear as bands. The plates are very obvious and delicately marked in oranges, browns, reds and occasional white patches. Underneath, the foot runs for most of its length, and down either side of the foot are gills that allow this quiet creature to obtain oxygen from circulating water.

RANGE: Southern California to Alaska

ZONE: intertidal; subtidal to 300 ft

HABITATS: quiet waters; rock; wood

LENGTH: to 2 in

COLOR: variable browns, reds

SIMILAR SPECIES: Lined Chiton (p. 109)

Lined Chiton
TONICELLA LINEATA

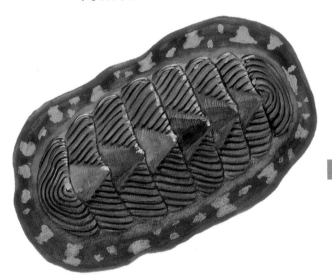

The Lined Chiton is the prize of the Pacific Coast and a feast for the eyes. Fortunately for us, it can occasionally be seen on rocks exposed at low tide, and close attention is required to pick it out. The chiton is so heavily lined with many colors that it blends surprisingly well with its environment, often avoiding detection. When the surge channels are quiet, be sure to look along the walls, as well as near patches of pink encrusting algae. This jewel of a chiton also turns up near the stunning Purple Sea Urchins (p. 135).

The patterns are highly variable and might involve just about every color of the rainbow. Most are reddish, with a smooth girdle blotched in creamy colors. The eight plates running down the back are busily lined in purple, black, white, pink, red, yellow and many other colors, depending on the individual chiton and where it has chosen to live. These chitons creep about the rocks consuming algae and anything growing on the algae, and are themselves the target of the Ochre Sea Star (p. 126).

RANGE: Southern California to Alaska

ZONE: lower intertidal; subtidal to 180 ft

HABITATS: rocky shores

LENGTH: to 2 in

COLOR: highly variable, mostly reddish

SIMILAR SPECIES: Merten's Chiton (p. 108)

Mossy Chiton

MOPALIA MUSCOSA

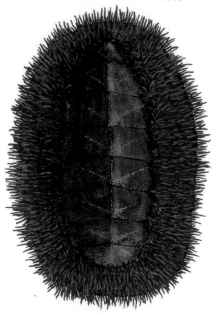

A thick, brown girdle covered in bristly hairs gives this chiton a mossy texture and appearance. The Mossy Chiton also comes in gray-green hues. The dark plates, exposed down the middle of its back, will sometimes have a pale line down the middle. This line is often obscured by an overgrowth of organisms that have made the chiton's back their home. Tubeworms, algae and barnacles are just some of the many organisms that you might find hitching a ride.

RANGE: Southern California to Alaska

ZONE: upper to lower intertidal

HABITATS: rocky shores; tidepools; estuaries

LENGTH: to 3.5 in

COLOR: brown, gray-green

This species is a common chiton found between the tides on rocky shores. Its ability to tolerate low salinity allows it to venture into estuaries as well. The Mossy Chiton makes a home on a favorite patch of rock. It never roams too far, and after a night of foraging and scraping away for food on the surface of rocks, it will return to its favorite spot. This chiton is just one of many different species of *Mopalia* chitons on the West Coast, many of which become luckless victims of the hungry attentions of the conspicuous Ochre Sea Star (p. 126).

California Nuttall's Chiton

NUTTALLINA CALIFORNICA

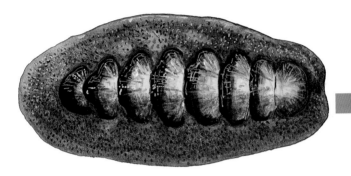

This darkly colored chiton often comes with a camouflaging overcoat of algae growing on its back. Some of these chitons lack this algae, and the plates down the middle of the back can be seen. When eroded, especially with older chitons, these plates appear pale, and the chiton might be confused with the Conspicuous Chiton. However, the girdle surrounding the plates on the California Nuttall's Chiton is proportionally much larger, and the Conspicuous Chiton grows to a greater size.

This chiton doesn't move much. It will often have a 'home scar' that it has worn away with its teeth. When the tide is out, the chiton returns to this little depression, and patiently waits for the tide to come back in and darkness to fall before roaming slowly about for Coralline Algae (p. 198). It will also feed on bits of seaweed that settle near its patch. This chiton favors the upper intertidal zone of exposed coasts, and can often be found nestled in barnacle and mussel beds. Some of these chitons can live for as long as 20 years, always grazing the same patch of turf.

RANGE: Southern California to British Columbia

ZONE: upper to middle intertidal

HABITATS: barnacle and mussel beds; rocky shores; exposed coasts

LENGTH: to 2 in

COLOR: dark brown, greenish

SIMILAR SPECIES: Conspicuous Chiton (p. 112)

Conspicuous Chiton

STENOPLAX CONSPICUA

The Conspicuous Chiton is particular about its habits, so be sure to look under intertidal rocks that are partially buried by sand. Here, the chiton is resting during the day and waiting for night to fall when it will become active by crawling about the rock looking for pieces of algae to eat. If its rock is overturned, this chiton will be upset by the intrusion into its home, and will crawl to the nearest dark place it can find. The largest of Southern California's chitons, Conspicuous Chiton grows to 4.5 inches and sometimes more.

RANGE: from Santa Barbara south

ZONE: middle to lower intertidal

HABITATS: under partially buried rocks

LENGTH: to 4.5 in

COLOR: greenish, blue, pink

SIMILAR SPECIES: California Nuttall's Chiton (p. 111)

Like all chitons, a series of plates, or valves, line the back. These valves are greenish-blue and often pink at the top where they have been eroded to reveal the soft colors inside. These smooth articulating plates are surrounded by a scaly girdle. Underneath is a huge foot. A tiny mouth conceals a serrated radula. This radula is comparable to a line of teeth used to graze on algae deposited on its home rock. The radula has deposits of magnetite made by the chiton, making the mouthpart very durable and an excellent grazing machine.

Yellow-edged Cadlina

CADLINA LUTEOMARGINATA

This whitish nudibranch is delicately fringed in bright yellow, and each tubercle on its back is tinged in yellow. Look under rocks and in tidepools near the low-tide line. This nudibranch is very similar to the Yellow-spotted Cadlina (*Cadlina flavomaculata*) that also has a yellow margin and spots. The rhinophores, however, are darker. The reverse coloration, a yellowish body with white dots, occurs in the common White-spotted, or Salted, Doris (*Doriopsilla albopunctata*).

When gently touched, the surface of the sea slug feels very rough. This texture is created by tiny spicules that are derived from sponges, which use it in their skeletal matrix. The nudibranch eats the sponge and puts the spicules to good use, instead of excreting them. A spiky meal is much less appetizing to potential predators. Few creatures relish eating nudibranchs because they can smell bad, taste bad, feel too spiky, or are even armed with stinging cells. So, for the most part, nudibranchs can go about their business of eating uninterrupted.

RANGE:	Southern California to Alaska
ZONE:	lower intertidal; subtidal to 75 ft
HABITATS:	rocky shores; under rocks; tidepools
LENGTH:	to 3 in
COLOR:	whitish; yellow markings

Ring-spotted Doris

DISCODORIS SANDIEGENSIS

This appealing nudibranch comes boldly marked with dark leopard-like spots and rings set against a creamy base color. It is commonly found along the Pacific Coast on the sides of boulders, under ledges and where seaweed can offer some protection. In the north of its range, the Ring-spotted Doris tends to have more rings, while in Southern California the rings can be so few in number that they seem completely lacking. Some Ring-spotted Dorises are dark instead of cream, often in shades of chocolate-brown.

OTHER NAMES: Ringed Nudibranch; Leopard Nudibranch; *Diaulula sandiegensis*

RANGE: Southern California to Alaska

ZONE: lower intertidal; subtidal to 110 ft

HABITATS: rocky shores; crevices; seaweed

LENGTH: to 3.5 in

COLOR: cream to brown; dark spots

As with many nudibranchs, sponges are their favored food item, especially the encrusting Purple Sponge (p. 180). A rasping radula, inside the mouth on the underside of the slug, is used to bite away at the sponge. Tiny, hairy projections on the skin give a rough feeling to this mollusk, and the tuft of gills at the rear can be retracted inside. Each Ring-spotted Doris is both male and female, and after mating with another individual, the sea slug lays a curly ribbon of white eggs in protected nooks.

Opalescent Nudibranch

HERMISSENDA CRASSICORNIS

This flamboyant and common sea slug graces the entire Pacific Coast. A slender, elegant body has many hair-like projections (cerata) in bands down each side of the body. The foot is translucent and lined with white or blue. The cerata are beautifully and variably presented, with white, orange and brown markings—the brown is an extension of digestive glands from the gut. Most distinctive is the vivid orange line down the middle of the back; the rest of the colors and markings can be quite variable. The Pugnacious Aeolid (*Phidiana pugnax*) looks very similar but has shorter red cerata and no stripe.

Tidepools on rocky shores, mud flats and beds of Eelgrass (p. 201) that are near the low-tide line are all the haunts of this aggressive carnivore. These nudibranchs consume small anemones, bryozoans, sea squirts, worms and much more. They are even fond of taking a bite out of each other, perhaps in defense of a favorite feeding territory. When they consume prey with stinging cells, such as sea anemones, they store up the stinging cells in the ends of their cerata for their own defense.

OTHER NAMES: Long-horned Nudibranch; Hermissenda; *Phidiana crassicornis*

RANGE: Southern California to British Columbia

ZONE: lower intertidal; subtidal to 110 ft

HABITATS: rocky shores; tidepools; eelgrass beds

LENGTH: to 3 in

COLOR: variable, pale with orange markings

SIMILAR SPECIES: Elegant Aeolid (p. 116)

Elegant Aeolid

CORYPHELLA IODINEA

Few creatures come more beautiful than the Elegant Aeolid. Although it has a wide distribution up the Pacific Coast, the further north you go, the less likely you are to see this treasure. In rocky areas look along the low-tide line among kelp. Pilings are an excellent site for watching all kinds of marine life, and these feathery mollusks show up here, too. The nudibranch feeds on tunicates like Sea Pork (p. 182), as well as hydroids. If disturbed or anxious, the Elegant Aeolid will launch into open water and swim away with quick bends of its long, slender body.

OTHER NAME: *Flabellinopsis iodinea*

RANGE: Southern California to British Columbia

ZONE: low-tide line; subtidal to 110 ft

HABITATS: rocks; kelp; pilings

LENGTH: to 3.5 in

COLOR: purple and orange

SIMILAR SPECIES: Opalescent Nudibranch (p. 115)

This nudibranch has a bright purple body adorned with vivid orange, finger-like growths, called cerata, rising from its back. Close inspection of each of these fingers will reveal a dark brown line inside, which is an extension of the gut. Few animals can be confused with this nudibranch, except maybe the Opalescent Nudibranch with its bright and variable colors. They share a similar body plan, so be sure to read about the Opalescent Nudibranch before determining the identity of your find.

Sea Clown Nudibranch

TRIOPHA CATALINAE

Dazzling and comical, the Sea Clown Nudibranch can be seen in the tidepools of rocky shores. So bright and cheerful, it is hard to miss. The whitish body is covered in stubby protuberances, each of which is tipped in strong orange. The sensory rhinophores (tentacles) and the frilled ring of gills are also colorfully tipped. The head is broad and bears several branched and forward-pointing projections.

These sea slugs are most often about 1 inch in length, but can grow to an impressive 6 inches. Unlike many other nudibranchs with their tough and hardened skins, these ones are rather squishy and flimsy, and one could imagine that they would make delectable eating. However, these noticeable slugs are never touched, and happily cruise the tidepool unharmed—the brilliant orange might serve as a deterrent and warning that they don't taste good.

RANGE: Southern California to Alaska

ZONE: intertidal; subtidal to 110 ft

HABITATS: rocky shores; tidepools; kelp

LENGTH: to 6 in

COLOR: orange flecks on white

Many nudibranchs, in calm pools, have the talent of walking upside-down along the undersurface of the water. This ability saves them from having to deal with all the obstacles of a trip along the bottom. Touch them gently and they will rapidly sink.

Blue and Gold Nudibranch

HYPSELODORIS CALIFORNIENSIS

For many creatures of the ocean the need to avoid predators has led them to resort to camouflage. However, in the case of the bold and brilliant Blue and Gold Nudibranch, this brazen slug has colors so glorious that it flaunts them with a great confidence. These colors warn potential predators not to come too close, because the slug secretes bad-tasting chemicals.

The Blue and Gold Nudibranch is a dark blue that is attractively marked with vivid yellow blotches. Around the fringe of the foot and the back (or mantle), there is a pale blue border that extends around the front end of the slug. The rhinophores at the front and gills at the rear are also dark blue. Hunt for this treasure along the low-tide line of rocky shores. This slug favors encrusting sponges, which make up the bulk of its diet. Although its range extends north to Monterey Bay in Central California, it is most common south of Point Conception and is a treat reserved for Southern California beachcombers.

RANGE: Southern and Central California

ZONE: lower intertidal; subtidal to 95 ft

HABITATS: rocky shores; on sponges

LENGTH: to 2.5 in

COLOR: blue; yellow spots

Orchid Nudibranch

CHROMODORIS MACFARLANDI

One of the greatest rewards of beachcombing along the low-tide line, and with patient observation, are the wonderful sea slugs. Many of the nudibranchs of Southern California are so lovely that the region should boast a 'state sea slug' to celebrate its rich marine fauna! One of the best candidates would have to be the Orchid Nudibranch, with colors that rival some of the finest orchids of the world. Look along the low-tide line on rocks and sponges. North of Point Conception, these slugs are quite rare.

The Orchid Nudibranch is deep pink and violet, and there are three bold yellow stripes running down its back. These stripes might have a reddish border to them. The fringe of the foot and the mantle (the back of the slug) is whitish. The little garland of gills at the rear of the slug gather oxygen from the water. This sea slug can often be found dining on sponges. While searching for these glorious creatures, you might well come across the Blue and Gold Nudibranch (p. 118) that also feasts on sponges near the low-tide line.

OTHER NAME: Macfarland's Dorid

RANGE: Southern and Central California

ZONE: lower intertidal; subtidal to 75 ft

HABITATS: rocky shores; on sponges

LENGTH: to 1.5 in

COLOR: pink, violet; yellow stripes

Hopkin's Rose
HOPKINSIA ROSACEA

Few beachcombers will forget the first time that they meet the petite and pretty-in-pink Hopkin's Rose. This elaborate little find, barely an inch long, is strikingly colored, and with its long, wavy projections, it is no wonder that it got named after a flower. Although it can be found all the way up into Oregon, this nudibranch becomes scarce north of Monterey Bay. Look along rocky shores and in tide-pools near the low-tide line. At first sight, it might easily be mistaken for an anemone.

RANGE: Southern California to Oregon
ZONE: lower intertidal; subtidal to 18 ft
HABITATS: rocky shores; on or near Rosy Bryozoans
LENGTH: to 1.25 in
COLOR: pink

Pink is most definitely the color of the day for this nudibranch. It is pink all over, has a small ring of gills at the rear end that are dark pink, and it feeds on the pinkish Rosy Bryozoan (p. 178). Staying true to form, it even lays ribbons of pink eggs. The small, oval body is almost covered by the fleshy projections. However, these projections are not cerata, as they are with the Elegant Aeolid (p. 116), because they do not have an extension of the gut inside. The small ring of darker-colored gills at the rear helps this sea slug extract oxygen from the seawater.

Navanax
NAVANAX INERMIS

A full-grown Navanax is a disturbing sight to other slugs and snails. This sea slug is a predator with an appetite. Once it has caught a sniff of the mucus trail of another mollusk, it pursues it at speed, and then swallows it whole. The Navanax haunts the mud flats and eelgrass beds of quiet waters. Mollusks of Northern California can rest easy, because the Navanax is a resident of Southern and Central California as far north as Monterey Bay. Search the calm waters near the low-tide line when the tide is out, but remember when the tide turns, it races in at great speed over these flats.

The Navanax is a large sea slug, growing to an impressive 8 inches in length. The long body can be as much 2 inches wide, and is edged with wing-like extensions of the mantle. These extensions are fringed in bright orange or sometimes blue. Other splashes of electric blue are streaked and dotted on the dark velvety body. Like the neon lights of a city street, a host of bright colors line and dot the surface of this elaborate creature.

OTHER NAME: *Chelidonura inermis*

RANGE: Southern and Central California

ZONE: near low-tide line; subtidal to 25 ft

HABITATS: mud flats; eelgrass beds; quiet waters

LENGTH: to 8 in

COLOR: dark base; bright colored streaks

Brown Sea Hare
APLYSIA CALIFORNICA

O ne of the most exciting finds of the low-tide zone is the mighty Brown Sea Hare. Named for its vague resemblance to a hare, this massive mollusk occurs on a variety of shores, from sand flats to rocky tidepools. It can grow to 20 inches in length and weigh as much as 15 pounds. This mollusk is only distantly related to the true nudibranchs, or sea slugs, in this book, because it retains a small shell inside its huge body.

Mostly mottled, the sea hare comes in shades of brown, red and green. These colors come from its food source, various kinds of seaweed. The sea hare stores up some of these seaweed chemicals in its body to make it distasteful to predators, and when provoked by a curious beachcomber it releases a harmless purplish fluid or ink in the same manner as a distressed squid. A close relative is the Black Sea Hare (*Aplysia californica*). This species is occasionally encountered in low-tide line pools. It is borderline scary for a slug, reaching 30 inches in length and weighing a staggering 35 pounds!

RANGE: California

ZONE: lower intertidal; subtidal to 60 ft

HABITATS: eelgrass beds; sand flats; rocky shores; tidepools; protected shores

LENGTH: to 20 in

COLOR: brown, reddish, green; mottled

Two-spotted Octopus

OCTOPUS BIMACULATUS

Close inspection of crevices, rocks and kelp along the low-tide line might deliver a Two-spotted Octopus. This creature is sensitive and shy, and deserves our respect. Too many are caught and eaten, resulting in a decline in their numbers. Any rough handling of this octopus might result in a painful nip, although this reaction is rare, partly because its remarkable agility makes it hard to catch. On mud flats the almost identical Mudflat Octopus (*O. bimaculoides*) is more common.

These octopuses are both variably colored in mottled shades of green, brown, gray or even red. They are remarkable color changers, varying their color to match their habitat or possibly their mood. Beneath each bulbous eye is a large dark spot, and underneath all those arms is a sharp beak used to bite into prey such as fishes, crabs and snails. Once the prey is grasped by suckered arms and bitten, a poison is released that paralyses it, making it an easy meal to handle. When threatened, the octopus releases a cloud of ink, rather like the Brown Sea Hare (p. 122). This cloud distracts the predator or beachcomber, allowing the octopus to make a swift retreat.

RANGE: from San Luis Obispo County south

ZONE: low-tide line; subtidal to 160 ft

HABITATS: rocky shores; crevices; among kelp beds

ARMSPREAD: to 36 in

COLOR: variable brown, green, gray, reddish; mottled

Opalescent Squid
LOLIGO OPALESCENS

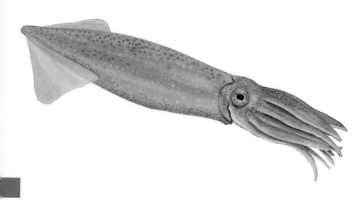

These squids are residents of the open seas, but come inshore to breed. They might be drawn to a nighttime light at the end of a pier. Egg cases are attached to the ocean floor, but are frequently cast ashore in great numbers. These egg cases look like 6-inch-long jellied sausages. Inspect them closely with a hand lens to see tiny baby squids (if they have had time to develop). Dead squids are often cast ashore at the same time. Aside from humans, squids are eaten by many animals, such as sea lions and some birds.

OTHER NAMES: Market Squid; Inkfish

RANGE: Southern California to British Columbia

ZONE: subtidal

HABITATS: open ocean; near kelp beds

LENGTH: to 12 in

COLOR: variable, often greenish

Eight arms and two armlike tentacles seize prey like small fish and crustaceans. The long, slender mantle ends with a triangular fin, and the squid is usually speckled. Close inspection will reveal many different pigmented spots in the skin, which the squid can alter at will and very quickly, too. This ability allows for rapid color changing, which often appears as a shimmering. Some pigments are pale green, giving the squid its opalescence. A distressed squid releases a cloud of ink, hence its other common name of 'Inkfish.'

124

Bat Star

ASTERINA MINIATA

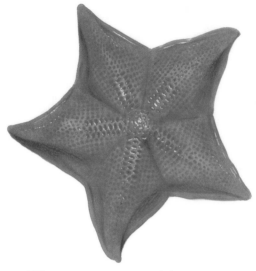

Wonderfully geometric with five stout arms, or rays, this sea star was once locally abundant in parts of California, but its distribution is now somewhat scattered. This decline in numbers is partly the result of losses in habitat from development of the coasts by humans. Where it does occur, its bright colors make it conspicuous against rocks and in tidepools. Once in a while the Bat Star will have more than five arms, sometimes as many as nine. It gets its name from its webbed arms, likened to a bat's wing. The commonest shades of these creatures include bright reds and oranges, as well as darker shades of green, brown and even purple, with mottling in some.

A Bat Star is not a fussy eater, happy to dine on almost anything. This sea star extrudes its stomach out of its mouth and wraps it around the food of its choice, digesting externally before swallowing. Algae and kelp are frequently consumed, but small animals do just as well. On the Bat Star's underside, look for the small, brown Bat Star Worm (*Ophiodromus pugettensis*) living in the grooves.

OTHER NAMES: Webbed Starfish; Sea Bat; *Patiria miniata*

RANGE: Southern California to British Columbia

ZONE: lower intertidal; subtidal to 950 ft

HABITATS: rocks; tidepools; open coasts

DIAMETER: to 8 in

COLOR: highly variable, red, green, brown, purple; mottled

125

Ochre Sea Star

PISASTER OCHRACEUS

The striking orange form of this sea star is a common sight on exposed, rocky shores. Clinging to wave-swept rocks, these rough-skinned sea stars are dark brown or purple; blunt, white spines give a coarse texture to the skin. A clean appearance is maintained by tiny pincers that peck and pull apart anything that lands on them. The sight or smell of this sea star is enough to send many intertidal organisms running, crawling, slithering or jumping for their lives.

Mussel and barnacle beds are the Ochre Sea Star's favorite domain—the appetite and abundance of which determine the lower limit of mussel beds. With its tube feet, the sea star gradually pulls the shells apart, inserts its stomach and slowly digests the contents—all of which can take a couple of days! These beauties are the sad victims of human ignorance. So hard and colorful are they that people take them home as beach souvenirs thinking they will dry up and look great on the mantlepiece. Instead, they rot and smell terrible, so please leave them where they belong.

OTHER NAMES: Pacific Sea Star; Purple Sea Star

RANGE: Southern California to Alaska

ZONE: intertidal; subtidal to 300 ft

HABITATS: exposed, rocky shores

DIAMETER: to 14 in

COLOR: orange-ochre, brown or purple

SIMILAR SPECIES: Giant Sea Star (p. 127); Short-spined Sea Star (p. 128)

Giant Sea Star

PISASTER GIGANTEUS

Close to the low-tide line, among rocks and sand, you might well catch a glimpse of the huge and chunky Giant Sea Star. Subtidally, this tough creature can grow to as much as 2 feet across, but is likely to be smaller (in the order of 8 inches) when found intertidally. A smaller Giant Sea Star might be confused with the more commonly found Ochre Sea Star, but the two are easy to tell apart. The Giant Sea Star always has white, evenly spread-out spines that do not form patterns in the same way as they do in the Ochre Sea Star. Each white spine is surrounded by a blue halo, a feature absent in Ochre Sea Stars. Giant Sea Stars come in base colors of brown, tan, reddish or sometimes purplish hues.

OTHER NAME: Knobby Starfish
RANGE: Southern California to British Columbia
ZONE: low-tide line; shallow subtidal
HABITATS: rocky shores; sandy areas
DIAMETER: to 24 in
COLOR: variable; with white spots circled with blue
SIMILAR SPECIES: Ochre Sea Star (p. 126)

Look for the Giant Sea Star in surge channels when the tide is out, where it might have come in on a feeding foray. But remember what dangerous places these channels can be when the tide is in. The Giant Sea Star prefers to dine on mussels, but will readily take other snails and bivalves, too.

Short-spined Sea Star

PISASTER BREVISPINUS

A long protected shores, tucked away among eelgrass beds and in quiet bays, the Short-spined Sea Star goes about its business. Its primary occupation is digging up clams and feasting on them. The mouth of the sea star is located in the middle of its body on the underside. Around the mouth, it has long, stretchy tube feet that it sends down through the sand to attach to clams and then pull them up. In quiet clearwater bays this species can sometimes be seen in abundance below the low-tide line.

OTHER NAME: Pink Sea Star

RANGE: Southern California to Alaska

ZONE: low-tide line; shallow subtidal

HABITATS: rocky shores; sandy areas; quiet bays; eelgrass beds

DIAMETER: to 24 in

COLOR: pink

SIMILAR SPECIES: Ochre Sea Star (p. 126)

While the Short-spined Sea Star prefers the soft sediments of quiet waters, it does also turn up on rocky coasts and on pilings. It is primarily a subtidal species, where it can reach impressive diameters of 2 feet. Shallower water individuals are usually much smaller, however. It is a soft, fleshy sea star, unlike its close relative, the Ochre Sea Star, which has tough and rugged skin. The Short-spined Sea Star might be confused with this other sea star, but it is always pink and seldom in the rough, exposed locations that the Ochre Sea Star enjoys.

Six-rayed Sea Star

LEPTASTERIAS HEXACTIS

This small sea star comes in shades of green to black, orange and tan, and is occasionally mottled, too. It requires some effort to find—look under loose rocks and boulders on the protected and open coast north of the Channel Islands. The Six-rayed Sea Star is distinct for having six rays, instead of the more normal five, and a feathery-looking texture from the closely packed spines. While searching, you might come across a brown sea star covered in orange spines and with only five arms. This sea star is the Soft Starfish (*Astrometis sertulifera*), which as its name implies is a soft and floppy creature.

OTHER NAME: Brooding Star
RANGE: from Channel Islands to British Columbia
ZONE: middle to lower intertidal; shallow subtidal
HABITATS: rocky shores; under rocks; tidepools; mussel beds
DIAMETER: to 3.5 in
COLOR: highly variable, black to mottled tan

The Six-rayed Sea Star is also called the 'Brooding Star' because of the female's unusual winter behavior. Standing on the tips of her rays, she creates a cavity for a mass of yellowish eggs, until they hatch. She then guards the tiny young until she feels confident that the baby stars can cling to the rocks on their own. After nearly two months of looking after her young, she can finally eat. This sea star eats mollusks—including the exquisite Lined Chiton (p. 109)—and barnacles.

129

Blood Star

HENRICIA LAEVIUSCULA

A dazzling splash of color to any dull rock is offered by the brilliant red Blood Star. It isn't always red, however. A younger, smaller Blood Star can be tan or even purplish and sometimes mottled. This species is an elegant sea star, with five long, slender rays and a very small central disk making this sea star look like it is all arms. Smooth to the touch, it has only very small spines.

OTHER NAME: Pacific Henricia

RANGE: Southern California to Alaska

ZONE: lower intertidal; subtidal to 1320 ft

HABITATS: rocky shores; encrusted rocks; tidepools; surge channels

DIAMETER: to 8 in

COLOR: variable, red, orange, tan, purplish; sometimes mottled

The Blood Star can grow to a diameter of 8 inches, but most are smaller.

Look for this splash of color on and under rocks. Small ones sometimes turn up in tidepools. Rocks covered in all sorts of marine encrusting organisms are favored, perhaps because the Blood Star prefers eating sponges. It also consumes tiny organisms, like bacteria, that settle and get trapped on its rays. The walls of surge channels are good places to look for it, but be cautious in surge channels. It's so easy to forget the clock when you are engrossed in the wildlife on the wall, and you might not notice the tide and strong waves marching their way in.

Panamanian Serpent Star

OPHIODERMA PANAMENSE

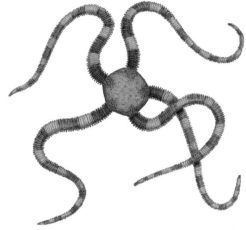

Brittle Stars have an eerie quality about them with their long, slender arms and writhing, wriggling antics—none more so than the Panamanian Serpent Star, because of its huge size as well. This brittle star is our largest, with a diameter of a foot, and sometimes more. This creature can be found under and between rocks in the middle and lower intertidal zone of most rocky shores. Most brittle stars will break apart when handled, but the Panamanian Serpent Star is a little more tolerant of handling, if those writhing arms don't put you off.

The central green-brown disk is pentagonal in shape, and an arm or ray extends from each corner. The rays are brown with paler bands and short, downward-pointing spines. These arms writhe about until they come into contact with suitable prey. Once contacted, the arm coils around it and the food is brought into the mouth located on the underside of the central disk. A diminutive version of this giant is Esmark's Brittle Star (*Ophioplocus esmarki*), which only grows to a diameter of 6 inches and there are even smaller species of brittle stars.

OTHER NAME: Snakeskin Brittle Star

RANGE: Southern California

ZONE: middle to lower intertidal; shallow subtidal

HABITATS: under and between rocks

DIAMETER: to 20 in

COLOR: brownish; paler bands

Spiny Brittle Star

OPHIOTHRIX SPICULATA

Tthis unmistakable brittle star is a common sight along the coast of California. Look among the rocks when the tide is out, in tidepools and in submerged crevices. Dense clumps of algae, especially in the holdfasts, and invertebrates are also favored locations for the Spiny Brittle Star. Here, it can firmly clasp its surroundings with some of its arms, while letting the others sway about in the currents, filtering the seawater for food.

The Spiny Brittle Star has five arms that are densely covered with long spines. The margin of the central disk is also fringed in spines. Each vicious-looking spine is itself covered in minute spinelets. The color is very variable, but is often orange and tan, with mottling. This brittle star also comes in various shades of green and brown. Whatever the color, it can always be recognized by the mass of spines. In deeper water, out of reach of the beachcomber, these brittle stars are known to gather by the million or more, which must be something of a creepy sight! Even inshore, where conditions are right, they will gather in big groups to feed.

RANGE: California

ZONE: lower intertidal; subtidal to 6600 ft

HABITATS: rocky and soft-bottomed shores; tidepools; holdfasts; invertebrate beds

DIAMETER: to 15 in

COLOR: variable orange, tan, brown or green

Eccentric Sand Dollar

DENDRASTER EXCENTRICUS

A popular souvenir of beachcombers, the flattened Sand Dollar is commonly found on sandy beaches. The familiar gray or white dollar represents the skeleton, or 'test,' of the urchin, which usually lives just below the low-tide line in sandy-bottomed areas. When living, the test is covered with tiny spines that give it a dark brown or purple color. Crowds of Sand Dollars can sometimes be seen vertically lodged in the sand filtering tiny particles from the water currents. Tiny hairs move the trapped particles towards the mouth.

In rough weather or at low tide, the Sand Dollar uses movable spines to bury itself further into the sand and flatten down so as not to expose itself to strong currents. Despite this activity, some will still end up stranded on the shore after a heavy storm. Here, they die and the spines are gradually washed away, revealing the characteristic five-petaled flower etched on the test, and hinting at the Sand Dollar's ancestral connection to sea stars. This off-centre pattern marks where the tube feet once emerged.

OTHER NAME: Sand Cookie

RANGE: Southern California to Alaska

ZONE: low-tide line; subtidal to 130 ft

HABITATS: sandy areas; sheltered bays

DIAMETER: to 3.25 in

COLOR: gray-white test; dark spines

Red Sea Urchin
STRONGYLOCENTROTUS FRANCISCANUS

Vibrant in color, the Red Sea Urchin, the giant of the West Coast urchins, has spines growing up to 3 inches long. This formidable-looking armory not only serves to protect, but also snares drifting fragments of algae, which are then gradually pulled apart and eaten. These scavengers eat all kinds of food, including dead fish, and they are found on open and sheltered rocky shores.

RANGE: Southern California to Alaska

ZONE: low-tide line; subtidal to 300 ft

HABITATS: rocky shores; open and protected coasts

DIAMETER: to 5 in without spines

COLOR: pink, red, reddish-purple

During the lowest tides along calm shores, wander down to the water and you might be fortunate enough to witness gatherings of these elaborate creatures.

Sea Otters (p. 31) are fond of urchins, and they can be seen pulling them apart on their bellies while floating on their backs. Where otters flourish, Red Sea Urchins do not. People who have developed a fascination for eating these sea urchins' ovaries are additional threats to them. Between the spines are tiny, pincer-like projections that pinch away at anything venturing too close. These 'pincers' can be enough—but not always—to scare off the hungry attentions of sea stars, but they are certainly no good against humans.

Purple Sea Urchin

STRONGYLOCENTROTUS PURPURATUS

Gorgeously colored in purple, this vibrant urchin is a resident of the exposed, rocky coasts. The Purple Sea Urchin is found in tidepools, and there is something of a mystery surrounding this relative of sea stars and sea cucumbers. Either with their five teeth or sharp spines, many Purple Sea Urchins end up in deep depressions in impossibly hard rock. It appears that they erode holes into the rock, and sometimes can never get out of them. Occasionally, they occur in such large numbers that the rock can be riddled with their burrows.

Algae are the main component of their diet, although some rock might be consumed (not that it has great nutritional value). Senior urchins, sometimes as old as 30 years, enjoy the exposed rocks, while the juveniles hide away in small crevices or mussel beds. Juveniles have greenish spines when less than 1 inch wide. The Purple Sea Urchin is much more common than the Red Sea Urchin in Southern California. Further north, however, the Red Sea Urchin can carpet the seafloor near the low-tide line.

RANGE: Southern California to Alaska

ZONE: middle to lower intertidal; subtidal to 30 ft

HABITATS: exposed, rocky shores; tidepools

DIAMETER: to 3.5 in without spines

COLOR: purple

Dwarf Sea Cucumber

LISSOTHURIA NUTRIENS

Sea cucumbers are definitely one of the more extraordinary features of the intertidal zone. Somewhat resembling a salad item, they are most definitely animal, and are related to sea stars and sea urchins. The Dwarf Sea Cucumber is as small as its name implies, barely reaching 1 inch in length, which is its greatest size. Look among algal holdfasts and in Surf Grass roots (p. 200) for these tiny but brightly colored sea cucumbers. They can also be seen stuck onto rocks, held tightly by three rows of tube feet on their flattened underside.

When feeding, a small crown of ten branching tentacles opens up around the mouth. These tentacles filter the seawater for tiny particles of food. Once a tentacle is sufficiently loaded, it is drawn into the mouth and wiped clean. This sea cucumber has the unusual habit of looking after its very young. It broods the young in pits on its back until they have tube feet strong enough to allow them to fend for themselves. Dwarf Sea Cucumbers might also have small pieces of algae stuck to their backs.

RANGE: Southern and Central California

ZONE: lower intertidal; subtidal to 65 ft

HABITATS: algal holdfasts; Surf Grass roots; encrusted rocks

LENGTH: to 1 in

COLOR: red

Warty Stichopus

PARASTICHOPUS PARVIMENSIS

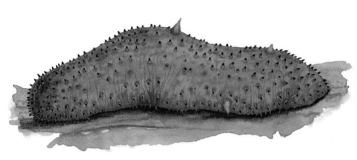

Sea cucumbers come in a range of sizes, from the tiny Dwarf Sea Cucumber (p. 136) to the huge Warty Sea Cucumber. This species is a regular find on rocky and soft-bottomed beaches at low tide. It is easy to identify, not least because of its large size, but also because of the mass of tiny, wart-like growths on its back, which are tipped in black. There might be one or two larger spines as well. The Warty Sea Cucumber is mostly a rich reddish-brown. It is widespread in Southern California and can be found as far north as Monterey Bay.

RANGE: Central and Southern California
ZONE: lower intertidal; subtidal to 100 ft
HABITATS: rocky and soft bottoms
LENGTH: to 10 in
COLOR: reddish-brown

Many sea cucumbers have a ring of tentacles that protrude around the mouth to catch particles from the water. This warty character lacks these tentacles, but picks up tasty deposits from the rock and sand by using tube feet around the mouth. Tube feet running along the underside of the cucumber move the floppy body around. Less common but just as large is the California Stichopus (*P. californiensis*). This cucumber is covered with many larger sharp warts or spines. There are several other smaller species to be encountered in Southern Californian waters

Purple-striped Pelagia

PELAGIA COLORATA

A number of jelly-like blobs will be stranded on the beach or get caught in a tidepool by the receding tide. Graceful in the open ocean, they become quite amorphous and helpless when plumped on the sand by a large wave. One striking arrival on beaches, and occasionally in tidepools, is the huge Purple-striped Pelagia, with a bell that is 30 inches or more wide and that has deep purple lines and dots. The tentacles hang from the fringe of the bell and have stinging cells called 'nematocysts,' which are used to catch prey. Steer clear of these nematocysts, because they are very toxic. This jellyfish moves inshore in late fall and winter.

OTHER NAME: Purple-banded Jellyfish

RANGE: California

ZONE: inshore; offshore

HABITATS: stranded on beaches

BELL DIAMETER: to 32 in

COLOR: translucent white and purple

Other jellyfish that are tossed ashore include the Moon Jelly (*Aurelia aurita*). This jelly has a translucent bell, with four horseshoe-shaped organs in the middle of the bell, which is only 15 inches across. Sometimes clouds of these jellyfish drift close to shore, and are washed up in great numbers. The similar-sized Sea Nettle (*Chrysaora melanaster*) is also frequently stranded here, and has pale brownish markings on the bell and dark-colored tentacles.

138

Sea Gooseberry
PLEUROBRACHIA BACHEI

After storms, beaches might be littered with glistening marble-sized blobs of jelly. These are the delicate Sea Gooseberries, open ocean-dwelling creatures that are at the mercy of the currents. If recently stranded and still alive, put them into a jar of seawater to see their tentacles unfold. Observe how the light plays over their surfaces. These animals belong in a group called the 'comb jellies,' named for the eight 'combs' that line the bulbous body. These combs are covered in small hairs, or cilia, that beat in rhythm, reflecting and defracting light, causing the beautiful iridescence of these creatures.

OTHER NAME: Cat's Eye
RANGE: California
ZONE: inshore; offshore
HABITATS: stranded on beaches
DIAMETER: to 1 in
COLOR: translucent white, iridescent

The Sea Gooseberry is less than an inch across, but has two long tentacles that trail behind it. These tentacles can be almost 6 inches long when fully extended, and are used to capture tiny floating animals (zooplankton). The tentacles are armed with sticky cells that ensnare the prey. When loaded with zooplankton snacks, the tentacle is retracted up to the mouth and the tentacle wiped clean. Because the animal is so transparent, you can faintly make out some of the organs inside.

By-the-wind Sailor
VELELLA VELELLA

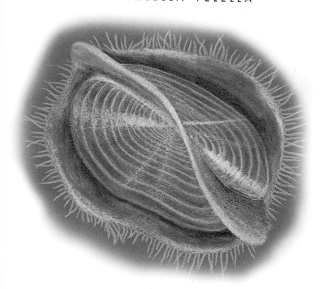

I n spring the beaches might be littered with the 4-inch-
long hard skeletons of the By-the-wind Sailor. This
bluish and translucent object is the remnant of a cnidar-
ian that once sailed the ocean. The unusual structure cast
ashore is filled with gas chambers that allow the animal to
float at the surface. The verti-
cal crest acts like a sail, and is
set at an angle to the length of
the body. This angled sail
allows the sailor to tack
against the wind, which works very well when the wind
blows from the north, but when it shifts to the west more,
the By-the-wind Sailor is driven ashore, sometimes in large
numbers.

RANGE: California
ZONE: inshore; offshore
HABITATS: sea surface; stranded
on beach
LENGTH: to 4 in
COLOR: bluish, translucent

A newly beached animal still has its fleshy parts, which
include a ring of tentacles that are used to feed on small
organisms swimming in the sea. After a few days, all the soft
tissue has decomposed and all that remains is the horny and
unique skeleton of the By-the-wind Sailor. After strong
winds, these remains can be piled up in banks along beaches.

140

Aggregating Anemone

ANTHOPLEURA ELEGANTISSIMA

Aggregating Anemones can be seen in profusion throughout much of the intertidal zone, whether smothering rocks in tidepools or on isolated rocks on beaches. To find them on surf-pounded beaches, look on the sheltered side of rocks that are protected from beating waves. When exposed, the elegant blue or pink stinging tentacles are withdrawn, and the anemones appear as greenish blobs of jelly. Sand and gravel often adhere in such quantities to the bodies of anemones that the anemones seemingly disappear.

A large aggregation, or colony, is formed by one anemone that has repeatedly divided, or cloned. Two colonies beside each other will have a small gap dividing them, as if they are intolerant of touching each other. When solitary, this anemone can reach much larger sizes. Its greenish color comes from tiny algae that are living in the host's soft tissues, just like the Giant Green Anemone (p. 142). A similar but solitary anemone that is found in sand near rocks is the Beach Sand Anemone (*Anthopleura artemisia*). It is actually attached to rocks beneath the surface, but keeps its crown level with the sand.

OTHER NAME: Elegant Anemone

RANGE: Southern California to Alaska

ZONE: upper to lower intertidal

HABITATS: rocky shores; tidepools

DIAMETER: to 2 in closed; 3.5 in open

COLOR: green body; variable tentacles

Giant Green Anemone
ANTHOPLEURA XANTHOGRAMMICA

The stunning green form of this huge anemone is hard to miss on open, rocky coasts. Shining away in tidepools and surge channels, this anemone enjoys a rough ride from the waves. Its brilliance comes from a colony of algae growing inside the translucent flesh; here, the algae are provided with a home and offer some nutrition in return. If deprived of light, the algae can die, and the anemone loses its magnificent color. In shaded tidepools, the anemone is a paler green because there are fewer algae inside.

RANGE: Southern California to Alaska

ZONE: lower intertidal; subtidal to 50 ft

HABITATS: rocky shores; tidepools; surge channels

DIAMETER: to 10 in

COLOR: variable greenish-blue

The tentacles are armed with tiny cells that each have a miniature harpoon. If you brush your hand across the tentacles, they feel sticky—this sensation is the tiny harpoons trying to drag you in. Once some prey is caught, the tentacles pass it into the mouth in the middle of the anemone, and the food is then digested. Anything that is not usable is then ejected out of the same hole. This anemone is often positioned where it can catch mussels that have been dislodged by rough surf.

Proliferating Anemone

EPIACTIS PROLIFERA

Petite and pleasing to look at, these delicate anemones come in a variety of colors in variable shades of red, green and brown. In rocky situations, they tend to be pink or red, while on Eelgrass (p. 201) or algae they are green or brown. White stripes radiate from the Proliferating Anemone's mouth and mark the column. This anemone can often be found in small gatherings in tidepools and at the base of rocks usually along the open coasts and in bays. It is widespread along much of the Pacific Coast.

The odd breeding behavior of this anemone is worth noting. Eggs are fertilized inside the cavity, and then the tiny young move out of the mouth, slide down the side of the anemone, and settle on the wide column. Here, the young will stay until they are large enough to fend for themselves. They don't wander too far, staying close to the parent and forming large patches of individual anemones. This squat anemone frequently suffers the predatory attentions of hungry nudibranchs.

OTHER NAME: Brooding Anemone

RANGE: Southern California to Alaska

ZONE: upper to lower intertidal; subtidal to 30 ft

HABITATS: rocky shores; tidepools; eelgrass beds; seaweeds

DIAMETER: to 2 in

COLOR: variable green, red, brown, pink

Club-tipped Anemone

CORYNACTIS CALIFORNICA

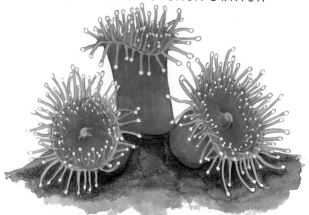

The Club-tipped Anemone is one of the prettiest anemones to be found in the low intertidal zone of California's open coastline and bays. It is small, about an inch big, and is most often in red or pinkish shades. Each tentacle is swollen and whitish at the end, hence its other name of 'Strawberry Anemone.' The Club-tipped Anemone also comes in shades of orange, purple or a ghostly white. Look among rocks, under ledges and on pilings for colonies of this creature. While inspecting pilings in harbors, you might find instead some brown-stemmed, white-tentacled Frilled Anemones (*Metridium senile*), although these are more common to the north.

OTHER NAME: Strawberry Anemone

RANGE: California

ZONE: low intertidal; subtidal to 150 ft

HABITATS: open coast; bays; rocky shores; tidepools; pilings

HEIGHT: to 1.25 in

DIAMETER: to 1 in

COLOR: red, pink, purple, orange, white

The swollen tentacles of Club-tipped Anemone contain the largest stinging cells of any anemone. Although they are not harmful to us, these tentacles are lethal to the small organisms that swim by. Colonies of these anemones are made by their remarkable ability to repeatedly divide, or split, down the middle—an easy way to reproduce. This anemone is, in fact, more closely related to Orange Cup Coral (p. 146) than to the other anemones described in this book.

White-spotted Rose Anemone

URTICINA LOFOTENSIS

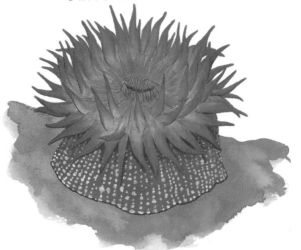

Once in a while the stunning White-spotted Rose Anemone makes its presence known in Southern California, although it is seldom found south of the Channel Islands. This brilliant red anemone grows to about 4 inches in diameter, and is easily identified by the neat rows of white dots on its column. Because of these dots, this anemone has also gone by the name of 'Strawberry Anemone,' a common name it shares with the Club-tipped Anemone (p. 144). The tentacles are scarlet, often with orange bases.

The best places to look for the White-spotted Rose Anemone are the rocky walls and floors of surge channels at low tide and on pilings. Surge channels are wild places, and the walls are often teeming with life that enjoy the rough surf and full force of the waves. Don't get too engrossed in the wildlife encrusted on the walls—always keep one eye open for the turning tide and the strong waves ready to rush up the channel. This anemone has the advantage of an extremely secure footing to prevent being washed away.

OTHER NAMES: Strawberry Anemone; *Tealia lofotensis*

RANGE: Southern California to Washington

ZONE: lower intertidal; subtidal to 75 ft

HABITATS: open coast; rocky shores; surge channels; pilings

DIAMETER: to 4 in

COLOR: red; white dots

Orange Cup Coral

BALANOPHYLLIA ELEGANS

The closest thing we have to the incredible coral reefs of the tropics is this tiny cup coral. The Pacific waters are too rough and cold to support anything more exciting in this region, and intertidally, this coral is the only one we will see. A little work is required to find it, because it often prefers the darker overhangs of ledges that are very close to the low-tide line. Here, it is not at risk of drying out, because it is protected from direct sunlight and uncovered for only a short time.

RANGE: Southern California to Alaska

ZONE: lower intertidal; subtidal to 160 ft

HABITATS: tidepools; crevices; overhangs; surge channels; open coast

DIAMETER: coral cup to 0.4 in

COLOR: orange

The Orange Cup Coral, when exposed at low tide, looks like a sharp and calcareous cup, with radiating walls inside and a tint of orange. In tidepools the delicate, translucent creature emerges from its stony home, spreading its faintly orange tentacles to catch and sting small prey. This coral is related to sea anemones, differing in that it builds a solid coral base to withdraw into. Other cup corals can be found at greater depths, but well out of reach of the beachcomber.

Yellow Crab

CANCER ANTHONYI

Cancer crabs, or rock crabs, are some of the largest of the West Coast crabs, and the ones most desired by commercial and recreational fisheries for their market value. In Southern California, it is the unfortunate Yellow Crab that is the most important contributor to the industry. This dusky yellow or orange crab has a broad, domed carapace, and the very tips of its claws are black. You might come across young Yellow Crabs under rocks in the intertidal zone from the San Pedro Channel south, but as they grow they move into deeper waters, preferring sandy bottomed areas of the Southern Californian coastline.

A number of other similar rock crabs occur in the region, including the Red Crab (*C. productus*), which is red as its name implies. Also, there is the Pacific Rock Crab (*C. antennarius*), which has reddish spots on its underside, a feature lacking in the uniformly colored Yellow Crab. Carapaces of all these crabs can often be found cast ashore. These carapaces do not mean that the crabs have died, but that they have been growing, shedding their older small carapace for a larger newer one.

OTHER NAME: Rock Crab

RANGE: Southern California

ZONE: lower intertidal; subtidal to 140 ft

HABITATS: rocky shores; under rocks; offshore sandy areas

WIDTH: carapace to 7 in

COLOR: tan, yellowish, orange

Swimming Crab
PORTUNUS XANTUSII

The Swimming Crab is all spines and jointed legs, and the large spines at the outermost edge of the cara- pace are the most distinguishing features. The last pair of legs at the rear are flattened into paddles to make this crab a very competent swimmer. It is most often a bluish-gray, with reddish or purple markings on the claws and legs.

RANGE: from Santa Barbara south

ZONE: lower intertidal; subtidal to 600 ft

HABITATS: sandy areas; quiet bays; eelgrass beds

WIDTH: carapace to 3 in

COLOR: bluish-gray; red or purple on legs

This aggressive predator comes inshore with the tide to hunt for prey, including other crabs. When the tide recedes, it is sometimes stranded and will bury itself in sand to wait for the next high tide. It can also be seen cruising about eelgrass beds in quiet-water bays. As an animal drifts by, the Swimming Crab swims up and seizes it in its vicious claws. Don't be tempted to mess with this crab. If the sight of all those spines doesn't put you off, then a painful pinch from the claws certainly will. Remember that this crab has claws that are strong enough to break through other crabs!

Striped Shore Crab

PACHYGRAPSUS CRASSIPES

This crab is versatile and adaptable, and you might come across it anywhere from rocky shores to the salty tidal creeks in estuaries. Gently turn rocks on sand over to see if you can find this crab. In tidal creeks, look for its burrow along the soft, sandy banks. This shore crab is variably colored, sometimes reddish, other times black, but it usually has green stripes running across the squarish carapace, and one spine is located behind each eye on the carapace. Two other crabs have the same body plan. The Purple Shore Crab (*H. nudus*) is most often purplish in color and has wonderful purple spots on its claws, and the pale Yellow Shore Crab (*H. oregonensis*) is found in quiet bays and estuaries.

RANGE: Southern California to Oregon
ZONE: upper to middle intertidal
HABITATS: rocky shores; bays; mussel beds; estuaries; tidal creeks; pilings
WIDTH: carapace to 2.5 in
COLOR: red, brown, black, green; green stripes

The Striped Shore Crab is a scavenger, feasting on pieces of seaweed, but it is occasionally more predatory, dining on limpets. Sometimes they can be observed rapidly scooping up tiny algae with their huge, spotted and striped claws. Get too close, and the crab will boldly present itself, claws outstretched, to encroaching beachcombers. When it realizes just how big you are, it scurries away.

Shield-backed Kelp Crab

PUGETTIA PRODUCTA

This elegant crab has an attitude, so if you are tempted to pick one up, be warned, because the long legs and claws can reach much further than the average crab. The smooth but sharply spined carapace comes in various shades to match the sea-weed on which the crab lives and dines—olive-green to reddish-brown shades are flecked with darker spots. Long limbs help these crabs grasp onto swaying kelp fronds.

RANGE: Southern California to Alaska

ZONE: lower intertidal; subtidal to 240 ft

HABITATS: rocky shores; kelp beds; tidepools

WIDTH: carapace to 3.75 in

LENGTH: carapace to 4.75 in

COLOR: variable reddish, brown, olive-green

Watch for them in seaweeds that wash back and forth in the surf. Sometimes an orange-brown crab will turn up in emerald Surf Grass (p. 200), in striking contrast.

The younger Shield-backed Kelp Crabs are inter-tidal, hidden under rocks and in tidepools. As they age, they tend to move into deeper water and kelp beds. In summer they will dine on kelp, but in win-ter, when much of the kelp has died, they become carnivores, extending their diet to barnacles and other intertidal organ-isms. Among low-tide line kelp, you might also find the Globose Kelp Crab (*Taliepus nuttalli*), which looks similar but has a rounded carapace and is not so shiny.

Nine-toothed Pebble Crab

CYCLOXANTHOPS NOVEMDENTATUS

Nestled between and under rocks in the middle to lower intertidal zone is the Nine-toothed Pebble Crab. This crab is brown or red, but can sometimes be found in bright purple hues, too. The crab can be identified by the nine rounded teeth on the edge of the carapace and the blackish claws. Although it can be found as far north as Monterey Bay in Central California, this large crab is only common in the southern-most counties of Southern California.

Younger crabs are found higher up the shore, often among small rocks, while older, larger crabs are found near the low-tide line. Here, they are known to excavate burrows under rocks. These crabs eat a variety of things, but are not averse to pulling apart a Purple Sea Urchin (p. 135) or to cracking open smaller crabs like the Lumpy Pebble Crab (p. 152). Most of their feeding activities are nocturnal, so some careful searching might be required to find these crabs during the day. If you do find one, the Nine-toothed Pebble Crab will play dead, hoping that you will leave it alone.

RANGE: Southern and Central California

ZONE: middle to lower intertidal; subtidal to 240 ft

HABITATS: rocky shores; under and between rocks

WIDTH: carapace to 3.75 in

COLOR: red, brown, purple

Lumpy Pebble Crab

PARAXANTHUS TAYLORI

While turning rocks and stones, keep an eye out for the tiny Lumpy Pebble Crab. This crab is somewhat secretive, and will often be hiding in holes in the underside of the rock you have just turned over. Don't try to pry it out with a sharp object, because you will most likely injure the creature. Instead, gently replace the rock exactly as you found it, so that the wildlife can resume their usual habits. Beachcombers in the southernmost counties are more likely to encounter the Lumpy Pebble Crab, because it is scarce to the north.

RANGE: Southern and Central California

ZONE: middle to lower intertidal; subtidal to 328 ft

HABITATS: rocky shores; under rocks; gravel; in kelp holdfasts

WIDTH: carapace to 1.5 in

COLOR: reddish-brown

This crab is easy to identify. It is a uniform reddish-brown with brown claws that have the appearance and texture (albeit on a small scale) of chocolate-coated nut clusters. The small legs to the rear are quite hairy, and the carapace is also lumpy. This crab is one of the easiest small crabs to identify. Smooth crabs of the same size will likely belong to the Mud Crab group (Lophopanopeus spp.) that like to raise their claws to ward off beachcombers. Small crabs with comparatively huge claws are likely the porcelain crabs (for example, p. 153).

Porcelain Crabs
PETROLISTHES SPP.

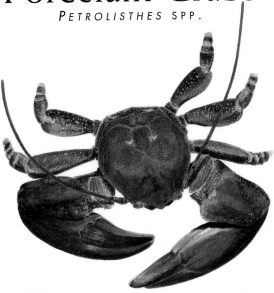

When you turn rocks on any California beach, the tiny crabs that scuttle away are likely to be porcelain crabs. The crab illustrated above is the Flat Porcelain Crab (*Petrolisthes cinctipes*), which can be found from Santa Barbara north. The rounded carapace is barely 1 inch in length, and the crab is usually quite drab in its various shades of brown (and occasionally blue). The long antennae are a deep red, and the claws seem enormous compared to the size of the body. In counting the legs you will discover it has only four pairs, while most 'true' crabs have five pairs.

RANGE: California to British Columbia
ZONE: intertidal
HABITATS: under rocks; stones; mussel beds
LENGTH: carapace to 1 in
COLOR: browns

Most porcelain crabs are filter feeders, sifting through the water for tiny particles of food. They can be very flat, which is an advantage when trying to squeeze into crevices or nooks on rocks. Beds of California Mussel (p. 92) are good places to poke around for porcelain crabs. If a crab fails to hide in a protective niche and is caught by a limb, it will happily autotomize, or shed, that leg in order to escape. The lost leg soon regrows, so it is not a major loss to the crab. The 'porcelain' name came from these crabs' apparent brittleness. Other small crabs include the Lumpy Pebble Crab (p. 152).

California Fiddler Crab

UCA CRENULATA

Be sure to wander along the high-tide line of estuaries and calm bays where California Fiddler Crabs make their homes, or burrows, in the mud. Some of these burrows can be as much as 4 feet deep! These crabs are active when the tide is low, and can be seen scurrying about picking up recently deposited organic material, called detritus. Approach slowly. Being sensitive crabs, a perceived threat will soon send them scurrying for their burrows.

They are easy to identify with their small, squarish carapace, uniform brown coloration and eyes on long stalks. Males have an enormously enlarged claw, which they wave around frantically. This claw-waving attracts females, who lack this large claw; the huge claw is also used to battle with the competition—other males that come too close. These territorial and mating displays are well worth the wait when beachcombing. Unfortunately, this spectacle is becoming increasingly hard to come by because of our habit of digging up and building on this crab's prime habitat. This species is our only fiddler crab—most of them can only be found in the mud flats of the tropics.

RANGE: from Los Angeles County south

ZONE: high-tide line; upper intertidal

HABITATS: estuaries; tidal creeks; calm bays

WIDTH: carapace to 0.75 in

COLOR: brown

154

Blue-handed Hermit Crab

PAGURUS SAMUELIS

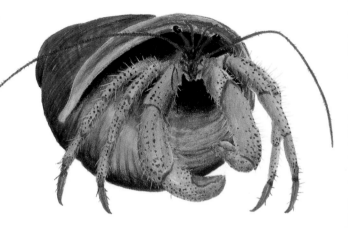

With their unusual preference for living in snail shells and their shy habit of hiding away, hermit crabs are one of the most popular intertidal animals. One of the hermit crabs to be found is the Blue-handed Hermit Crab, the adult of which shows a distinct preference for the shells of the Black Tegula (p. 62). This hermit is olive to yellowish-green in color, and most distinct are the bright blue bands around the base of the legs. Its antennae are bright red. The carapace is striped and ends as a beak-like projection between the eyes. This projection and the bright blue band distinguish this hermit from the Little Hairy Hermit Crab (*P. hirsutiusculus*), which is found lower in the intertidal zone and has duller colors with some white banding on the legs.

OTHER NAME: Blueband Hermit
RANGE: Southern California to Alaska
ZONE: upper to lower intertidal; subtidal to 50 ft
HABITATS: open, rocky shores; tidepools
LENGTH: to 0.75 in
COLOR: olive-green to yellowish; blue bands

Hermit crabs have soft abdomens that they need to tuck away inside shells for protection. At the end of the abdomen is a hook-like tail that clings to the inside of the shell. As hermit crabs grow, they need to move into a larger shell. House-moving must be done quickly—the crabs are very vulnerable to attack at this time.

155

Pelagic Red Crab
PLEURONCODES PLANIPES

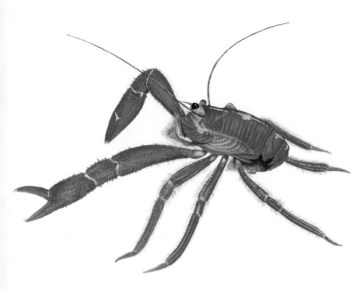

Once in a while you might go down to the beach, only to discover that it is smothered in hordes of the Pelagic Red Crab. 'Pelagic' means that this crab is normally a resident of the open sea. Its approximate and usual home is in the open ocean west of Mexico. During an El Niño year (see p. 20), however, warm water moves up from the south, bringing these crabs along for the ride. When conditions are right, and the winds drive surface seawater to shore, the crabs get stranded in vast numbers and die. This certainly makes for rich pickings for all the scavengers of the intertidal zone!

OTHER NAMES: Squat Lobster; Tuna Crab; Lobster Krill
RANGE: Southern California
ZONE: offshore
HABITATS: stranded on beaches
LENGTH: carapace to 2 in
COLOR: bright red
SIMILAR SPECIES: California Spiny Lobster (p. 157)

This crab goes by a number of names, including 'Tuna Crab' because it is a favorite food of the fast-swimming tuna fish, and 'Lobster Krill,' because of its resemblance to a lobster. It is bright red in color, with faint stripes on the carapace and long, slender claws and legs. It feeds on tiny animals suspended in water, and is itself an important contributor to the food chain, being eaten by large fish and sea mammals.

California Spiny Lobster

PANULIRIS INTERRUPTUS

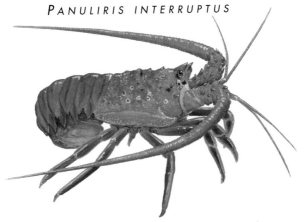

Many of us know what a lobster looks like on a dinner plate, because these luckless creatures are fished commercially. Being an expensive delicacy is something that few animals would seek if they knew what it entailed! For the lucky beachcomber, a glimpse of an intertidal California Spiny Lobster is still a possibility, but it won't be anywhere near as large as the restaurant giants, which weigh in as much as 30 pounds. Occasionally trapped in pools at low tide, the lobster will seek out a crevice or seaweed to hide in. Lobsters are reddish and very spiny, and instead of claws they have strong mouthparts that can crunch through tough animals.

If you are tempted to grab a lobster, then there are several reasons not to. Firstly, the thick, long antennae are covered in sharp spines that can inflict nasty cuts. Secondly, a small lobster will become a big lobster, so if you are a real lobster nut, letting it live for a few more years will bring a greater reward. Alternately, you might want to give it the chance to defy all the lobster trays and have a long life. If none of those reasons is enough to deter you, then state law restricts lobster harvesting by size, so check the current regulations.

OTHER NAME: Langosta

RANGE: Southern California

ZONE: lower intertidal; subtidal to 200 ft

HABITATS: rocky shores; under seaweed and rocks

LENGTH: to 30 in

COLOR: red, brown

SIMILAR SPECIES: Pelagic Red Crab (p. 156)

Acorn Barnacle
BALANUS GLANDULA

By far one of the most abundant animals to be found on rocky shores, these inconspicuous barnacles are easy to step over and ignore. Bend down a moment and study them! The Acorn Barnacle prefers the middle to upper intertidal zone where it is out of reach of many of the predatory snails. So resilient are barnacles that an occasional ocean spray keeps them alive. During scorching sun or heavy rain, these tiny crustaceans, which are related to crabs and shrimps, close up their impenetrable plates like doors.

OTHER NAME: Common Barnacle
RANGE: Southern California to Alaska
ZONE: upper to middle intertidal
HABITATS: rocky shores
DIAMETER: to 0.6 in
COLOR: gray-white

Various small acorn barnacles (*Chthamalus* spp.) are only a fraction of an inch across and are often seen growing next to the larger and paler Acorn Barnacle. The protective plates inside the 'crater' help identify which species you are looking at: small acorn barnacles, sometimes called Brown Buckshot Barnacles, have a religious cross on the plates, while the Acorn Barnacle has wavy edges. As the tide recedes, be sure to look into tidepools filled with barnacles, and watch for their frantically waving 'cirri'—hand-like projections—that grasp for any tiny food particles left by the receding waters.

158

Giant Acorn Barnacle

BALANUS NUBILIS

Near the low-tide line of open coasts, it is possible to see this massive barnacle adhered to rocks, pilings or other hard surfaces. The Giant Acorn Barnacle is so large that the native peoples of the Northwest once ate it roasted. Sometimes the barnacles grow in bunches, on top of one another, until the mass becomes so thick and unstable that a storm can break it off at the base. Each barnacle is made from rough outer plates that are frequently encrusted with many different organisms. The inner plates are pointed and protect the 'cirri,' hand-like projections, that come out to catch particles of food when the tide is in.

RANGE: Southern California to Alaska

ZONE: lower intertidal; subtidal to 300 ft

HABITATS: rocky shores; exposed coasts

DIAMETER: to 4 in

COLOR: gray-white plates; pinkish flesh

A barnacle is much like a shrimp that has landed on its head and built a wall around itself. This barnacle is almost as high as it is wide, and when the animal dies, the cavity left behind makes an ideal home for many organisms. Some crabs will take up residence inside. An even larger barnacle is the Eagle Barnacle (*B. aquila*), growing to 5 inches or more.

Volcano Barnacle

TETRACLITA RUBESCENS

One of the most attractive barnacles to be found in Southern California is the Volcano Barnacle. Looking very much like an idealized volcano, this sizable barnacle is found in the intertidal zone, from middle to lower levels, on rocky shores of the exposed coast. It is distinctive with its reddish hues, and the ribs run down the sides of the barnacle, much like the lava streams on a volcano.

OTHER NAME: Thatched Barnacle

RANGE: Central and Southern California

ZONE: middle to lower intertidal

HABITATS: rocky, exposed shores; surge channels; overhangs; pilings

HEIGHT: to 2 in

DIAMETER: to 2 in

COLOR: reddish

SIMILAR SPECIES: Red-striped Acorn Barnacle (p. 161)

Look in the surge channels and under overhangs for the Volcano Barnacle. It prefers the shadowed, darker corners of the intertidal world, and can sometimes be seen on encrusted pilings. When the tide is out, four plates seal off the animal inside from the predators and dryness of the outside world. As waves splash over and cover them, the plates are opened, and a net of cirri is swept through the water to catch tiny particles of food. Once loaded, they are withdrawn into the barnacle and the food is removed and eaten. There are other reddish or pink barnacles to be found. Compare this one with the Red-striped Acorn Barnacle.

Red-striped Acorn Barnacle

MEGABALANUS CALIFORNICUS

Near the low-tide line of the rocky shores of Southern California, clusters and individuals of the Red-striped Acorn Barnacle can be seen. These barnacles are beautifully marked, as barnacles go. They are easy to identify with their red-and-white striped plates on the sides. These plates help form the hard walls protecting the soft flesh of the crustacean inside, tapering to a point at the crown of the shell. In between each striped plate is a whitish band with thin, horizontal lines. Most often, you will find these barnacles at low tide, exposed to air. Unfortunately, when they are closed up we don't get to see their striped and feathery appendages, or cirri, that are used to catch food from the water. Sometimes, the barnacles occur in tight clusters, forcing them to grow tall and thin.

RANGE: Central and Southern California

ZONE: lower intertidal; subtidal to 30 ft

HABITATS: rocky shores; pilings

DIAMETER: to 2 in

COLOR: red and white

SIMILAR SPECIES: Volcano Barnacle (p. 160)

There is another red barnacle that resembles the Red-striped Acorn Barnacle. This one is the Little Pink Barnacle (*Balanus amphitrite*), which is only 0.75 inches across, and can be found on rocks and shells in more protected waters. The Volcano Barnacle is also reddish, but does not have the distinctly separate and stripy plates of the Red-striped Acorn Barnacle.

Blue Goose Barnacle

LEPAS PACIFICA

After a storm, be sure to hike the sandy beaches for articles that have drifted in from the open seas. Aside from disheartening garbage, there is often driftwood sculpted by years in the ocean. Inside the wood are many Pacific Shipworms (p. 107), and outside are the strange Blue Goose Barnacles. These creatures can be found in large colonies on floating objects, including plastic and Styrofoam. The tiny nauplius (barnacle larva) swims in open waters until attracted to the shade of something floating—here it sticks for good.

RANGE: Southern California

ZONE: offshore; pelagic; open ocean

HABITATS: on floating objects; stranded on beaches

LENGTH: to 2.75 in

COLOR: black stalk; bluish shell

SIMILAR SPECIES: Leaf Barnacle (p. 163)

Blue Goose Barnacles are closely related to the hard-shelled barnacles stuck on rocks. A thick, fleshy stalk supports the crustacean. Smooth, white plates edged in red form a shell, and when submerged, the cirri (hand-like projections) are extended out to filter the water. The bluish color is the animal inside, which is visible through the thin plates. Baking sunshine soon kills these beached barnacles, and gasping barnacles with withered cirri can be seen hanging out of their home. Further to the north a common find is the Common Goose Barnacle (*L. anatifera*), which is almost identical, but grows to a length of 6 inches.

Leaf Barnacle

POLLICIPES POLYMERUS

Leaf Barnacles are frequently found on the exposed coast in thick clusters stuck amidst beds of California Mussel (p. 92). These peculiar bunches of crustaceans thrive in the pounding surf—surge channels and very exposed rocks being the favored locations. They differ from the Blue Goose Barnacle in that they stick to rocks on shore, and have many smaller plates protecting the animal inside.

The stalk is a deep reddish-black and covered in minuscule spines that are arranged in neat rows. These stalks are tough and rubbery to cope with the stress of stormy seas.

As waves break over the rocks, the barnacles open and stretch out their cirri to catch the backwash off the rocks. Their hope is to rake in any small organisms washed off their footings. When closed, dark red 'lips' mark where the cirri come out. If you pass your hand over the top so that your shadow passes over them, notice how they twist and retract a little bit. Why they do so is a mystery, but obviously they are light sensitive, or maybe a little worried that you might do them some harm.

OTHER NAME: Goose Barnacle

RANGE: Southern California to Alaska

ZONE: upper to lower intertidal

HABITATS: rocky shores; mussel beds

LENGTH: to 3.25 in

COLOR: dark stalk; whitish plates

SIMILAR SPECIES: Blue Goose Barnacle (p. 162)

Red Rock Shrimp
LYSMATA CALIFORNICA

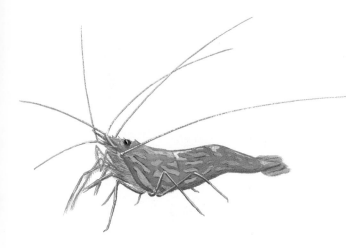

M any kinds of shrimp can be found in the tidepools of Southern California, and identification can be quite challenging. One of the more common and striking shrimps you will likely encounter is the Red Rock Shrimp. An excellent time to see this shrimp in action is at night. Shine a flashlight into tidepools to see these brightly colored shrimp scurry about. Other smaller shrimp you will encounter in tidepools include the many species of Broken-back Shrimps (*Heptacarpus* spp.), with their distinctive kink in the back.

RANGE: Southern California

ZONE: middle to lower intertidal; subtidal to 200 ft

HABITATS: rocky shores; tidepools

LENGTH: to 2.75 in

COLOR: cream and red

The Red Rock Shrimp is one of the easiest to identify. It is cream in color, with many red stripes that often merge making it look mostly red. The Red Rock Shrimp also has very long, red antennae. One of the more daring habits of this shrimp is that it cleans around the gruesome mouth of the California Moray (p. 50). The moray welcomes the picking and cleaning, because the shrimp removes parasites and small bits of dead skin. The Red Rock Shrimp will also happily service the dazzling Garibaldi (p. 47) and has been known to clean the fingers of divers.

Smooth Skeleton Shrimp

CAPRELLA LAEVIUSCULA

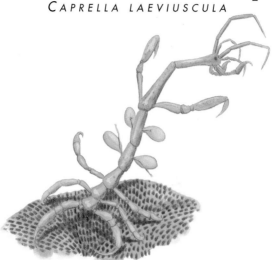

The peculiar and rakish Smooth Skeleton Shrimp clings to hydroids, such as the Ostrich Plume Hydroid (p. 179), Eelgrass (p. 201) and algae, on both rocky and sandy shores. The last three pairs of the shrimp's legs have hooks for feet, and these hooks help the creature grasp tightly and securely to its perch. From here, it waves gently back and forth, consuming tiny animals suspended in the water, pieces of algae and single-celled plants.

Although it carries the name 'shrimp,' this species is not a true shrimp, but belongs to a group of crustaceans called 'amphipods.' The highly jointed body bears numerous appendages and claws, and it comes in shades of green, tan or pinkish, depending on which color is the most suitable for camouflage. Occasionally, skeleton shrimps, of which there are a number of different species, can be seen clinging in clusters with their arms outstretched. Like strange beasts from another planet, these animals deserve some close inspection with a hand lens so that you can see their strange body shape and curious behavior.

RANGE: Southern California to British Columbia

ZONE: lower intertidal; shallow subtidal

HABITATS: eelgrass beds; algae; hydroids; rocky and sandy areas

LENGTH: to 2 in

COLOR: variable green, tan, pinkish

165

Harford's Greedy Isopod

CIROLANA HARFORDI

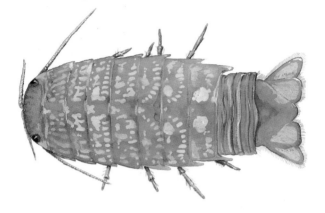

From the high- to low-tide line, Harford's Greedy Isopods are scurrying about on their many legs, often beneath rocks and seaweeds. These isopods (a type of crustacean) are the caretakers of the intertidal world. When a dead animal is cast ashore, you are sure to come across these greedy characters getting their fill by devouring the corpse. This behavior has earned them their rather unflattering name. The nooks in mussel beds are also great hiding places for these crustaceans. Many fish and other animals make these crusty snacks a staple in their diet, because they can be so abundant.

RANGE: Southern California to Alaska

ZONE: upper to lower intertidal; shallow subtidal

HABITATS: exposed and quiet rocky shores; under rocks; mussel beds; seaweed; tidepools

LENGTH: to 0.75 in

COLOR: brown, black, gray, tan; paler mottling

SIMILAR SPECIES: Western Sea Roach (p. 167)

Harford's Greedy Isopod is usually quite drab, colored in gray, tan, brown or black. There are two pairs of antennae on the head, and a fan-like tail to the rear. Its armored plating is frequently flecked with paler markings. A similar isopod that grows to almost 1.5 inches is Vosnesensky's Isopod (*Idotea wosnesenskii*), which shares many of the same habitats. This soft-looking isopod can come in a variety of colors, often brightly hued in pink and red to match with its habitat.

Western Sea Roach

LIGIA OCCIDENTALIS

Near and above the high-tide line, this cockroach-like creature stays tucked out of sight during the day. As the light fades, however, the Western Sea Roach crawls out from hiding in the cracks and crevices and starts to feed on the thin film of algae covering the rocks. By day, turn over a rock and you might well scare one or two of these roaches. They will run for cover in another sheltered spot.

Although these crustaceans prefer life at the limits of high tide, they are still dependent on the moisture of the sea; sometimes they can be seen crawling down to the edge of the tidepool where they dip their rear end into the water to moisten up the soft gills inside.

RANGE: Southern and Central California
ZONE: high-tide line and above
HABITATS: under rocks; crevices
LENGTH: to 1 in
COLOR: brown, tan, gray
SIMILAR SPECIES: Harford's Greedy Isopod (p. 166)

Western Sea Roaches can be found from Sonoma County in Central California south. You might confuse these crustaceans with Harford's Greedy Isopod. The roaches are a bit larger, with longer legs and antennae and long, thin appendages at the rear end instead of the isopod's fan-like tail. Western Sea Roaches will move faster, too.

California Beach Flea

MEGALORCHESTIA CALIFORNIANA

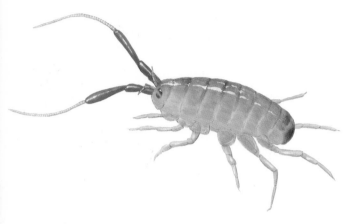

Amidst the wrack cast up on beaches at the high-tide line, thousands of small jumping creatures are tucked away. On sandy beaches north of Laguna Beach, many of these creatures are California Beach Fleas. By day, they rest and keep moist, either in their burrows or under mats of kelp decomposing on the shore. By night, they come out in the thousands to feast on the latest kelp delivery from the sea. The beach fleas follow the waves down the beach, and retreat before the tide comes in.

With a sandy-colored body and bright red antennae, these are attractive crustaceans. Younger individuals have darker patches down their back. Unfortunately, many people are put off by the sheer number of fleas and their writhing, jumping madness when disturbed. That they are called 'fleas' doesn't help their reputation at all, because California Beach Fleas do not bite. Strong back legs give them an enormous athletic talent for jumping, earning them their common name. South of Laguna Beach the beach fleas are a different species—the very similar Large Beach Hopper (*Orchestoidea corniculata*). It has proportionally shorter antennae.

OTHER NAME: *Orchestoidea californiana*

RANGE: from Laguna Beach north to British Columbia

ZONE: high-tide line and above

HABITATS: sandy beaches

LENGTH: to 1.1 in

COLOR: tan; red antennae

168

Tapered Flatworm

NOTOPLANA ACTICOLA

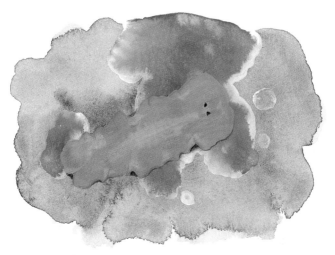

When looking under the rocks of the intertidal zone, you are likely overlooking the common Tapered Flatworm, because it resembles more of a thin film of goo than a living animal. Sometimes it is so thin that it appears to be translucent. Usually the color of the Tapered Flatworm is tan or gray, sometimes mottled, with some noticeable eyespots nearer the broader front end. This flatworm also has eyespots around the edge of the body, but these are often too small to be seen with the naked eye. Being so flat, the flatworm is quite capable of crawling into minute crevices. By day, a flatworm will remain under rocks, but it will emerge and glide about at night.

RANGE: California
ZONE: upper to lower intertidal
HABITATS: under and on rocks; crevices
LENGTH: to 2.5 in
COLOR: tan, gray

Flatworms are an unusual group of worms. They have a big mouth on the underside, and with this mouth they tend to gulp down their prey. Tapered Flatworms will dine on small invertebrates, even limpets half their size. They can glide rapidly about using tiny hairs on their underside. A simple gut spreads down the middle of the worm, and the mouth must be used to excrete waste as well.

Green Nemertean

EMPLECTONEMA GRACILE

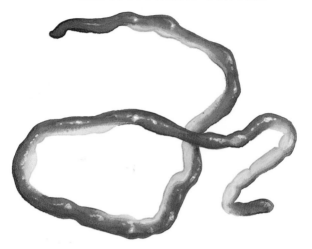

This nemertean, or ribbon worm, is an unusual but common find among mussel beds, algal growths or other well-covered, rocky surfaces in which it can crawl about. This worm's soft, green body is paler on the underside, and it can be very long and thin, sometimes as long as 20 inches, yet will only be a few inches when contracted. Despite this elasticity, the Green Nemertean is fragile because it is very thin, so please do not tug at it because it could fall apart in your hands. However, this isn't fatal to the worm, because each chunk of the broken worm becomes a new Green Nemertean. In quiet waters, you are more likely to find the Fragile Nemertean (*Cerebratulus californiensis*). Variably colored, it can be recognized by its flattened rear half.

RANGE: Southern California to British Columbia

ZONE: intertidal

HABITATS: rocky shores; mussel beds

LENGTH: to 20 in

COLOR: green above; pale below

All nemerteans are carnivores, with the disturbing habit of reversing the proboscis out of the head to catch prey. By squeezing a few muscles here and there, the pressure forces the sticky mouthpart out onto the prey. Armed with small arrows and venom, the prey is caught by the proboscis, and then usually swallowed whole.

170

Eighteen-scaled Worm

HALOSYDNA BREVISETOSA

This strange armored creature inhabits many corners of the intertidal zone, tucked away under algal hold-fasts or under tidepool rocks. It is very hardy, enjoying all kinds of conditions from the low-salinity waters of estuaries to the dark depths of 1460 feet. This worm, with 18 pairs of scales running down each side, also turns up in the tubes of other worms and the shells of hermit crabs, where it can grow to as much as 4 inches in length. The wandering species that a beachcomber is more likely to encounter can be as long as 2 inches. Its color is usually a gray-brown, with paler markings in each scale.

The scales down the back serve as a brooding chamber for the eggs, which are very easily dislodged; be careful if you are inclined to handle such creatures. These worms are carnivores and rather intolerant of their own kind—if confined in the same container, some scale worms will readily bite each other. Very similar and found in the same habitats is the Twelve-scaled Worm (*Lepidonotus squamatus*) and the Fifteen-scaled Worm (*Harmathoe imbricata*), both also growing to about 2 inches in length.

OTHER NAME: *Halosydna johnsoni*
RANGE: Southern California to Alaska
ZONE: middle to lower intertidal; subtidal to 1460 ft
HABITATS: tidepools; under rocks; holdfasts; mussel beds; in tubes of other animals
LENGTH: to 4 in
COLOR: gray-brown

Clam Worm
NEREIS VEXILLOSA

This bristly annelid worm occurs in mussel beds on the open coast and under rocks and driftwood in bays. During summer nights in quiet bays, these worms will often swarm and wriggle about in great numbers at the surface of the water to breed. This worm is segmented, and the bristly appendages on each segment help the worm move around. An individual is often encountered creeping its way about, looking for chunks of seaweed or animals to bite off with its strange mouth. The complex mouthpart comes right out of the worm's head, so that it can bite more successfully. If you find one, gently squeeze it behind the head and the mouthpart will emerge.

OTHER NAME: Mussel Worm
RANGE: California to Alaska
ZONE: intertidal
HABITATS: rocks; mussel beds; wood; quiet bays; open coast
LENGTH: to 6 in
COLOR: gray, with iridescence

The base color is mostly grayish, with an iridescence that gives the worm hues of green, pink or blue. This Clam Worm grows to about 6 inches in length. A smaller, similar *N. grubei* grows to 4 inches. A close relative, the Lug Worm (*Arenicola brasiliensis*) has taken to burying itself in mud of quiet bays—the muddy casts left at low tide are the evidence.

Red Tube Worm
SERPULA VERMICULARIS

When you turn rocks at low tide, you might overlook a dead-looking crusty tube. This calcareous tube, often covered with marine growth, is home to the Red Tube Worm, and is well worth further investigation. When immersed in water, a brilliant display of red gills is pushed out of the sinuous tube. There are 40 pairs of gills with which the worm feeds and breathes. The body of the worm is tucked safely away inside the tube. Some worms have pink gills; others are banded in white.

Any firm surface covered with water makes a good home, and the distinctive tubes turn up on pilings and shells. When the feeding worm is disturbed, the gills are withdrawn in a flash and the entrance to the tube is sealed off with a red, funnel-shaped operculum. Empty tubes are obvious because they lack this bright red door. Similar but minuscule by comparison is the Tiny Tube Worm (*Spirorbis borealis*), which is commonly found on hard surfaces immersed in water and grows to a mere eighth of an inch.

OTHER NAME: Calcareous Tube Worm

RANGE: Southern California to Alaska

ZONE: lower intertidal; subtidal to 300 ft

HABITATS: under rocks, shells, pilings

LENGTH: to 4 in

COLOR: white tube; red, pink or whitish gills

SIMILAR SPECIES: Scaly Worm Shell (p. 174)

Scaly Worm Shell

SERPULORBIS SQUAMIGERUS

Individuals and colonies of scaly, hard tubes are a frequent sight attached to intertidal rocks. Because of their strong resemblance to worms, such as the Red Tube Worm, the Scaly Worm Shell has been placed in this section of the book. You can be forgiven for thinking that this creature is a worm, when it is, in fact, a mollusk. Think of it as a snail with a shell that has unraveled, instead of being kept coiled in a tidy spire.

RANGE: Southern and Central California

ZONE: upper to lower intertidal; subtidal to 65 ft

HABITATS: attached to rocks, pilings; bays; estuaries; open coast

LENGTH: to 5 in

COLOR: whitish, gray

SIMILAR SPECIES: Red Tube Worm (p. 173)

The Scaly Worm Shell can be found on rocks in many locations, from surge channel walls to rocks in the calm of bays. The texture is rough, often scaly, helping distinguish it from the Red Tube Worm. Also, instead of a head of feathery appendages filtering the water, this mollusk sends out strands of mucus on which tiny particles of food get trapped. This mucus is then eaten. On rocks in the intertidal zone another creature builds tubes in great numbers—the Sand Castle Worm, but these colonies of worms can be more organized than the twisting, turning masses of the Scaly Worm Shell.

Sand Castle Worm

PHRAGMATOPOMA CALIFORNICA

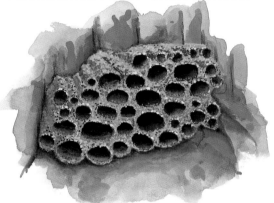

On intertidal rocks, an astonishing mass of tube worms can be found. These are the Sand Castle Worms. A large colony has been likened to a honeycomb, because the worms can be neatly arranged. Big colonies can be as much as 6 feet across. Each worm, however, is much smaller, only 2 inches long with a small opening. The colonies can be seen on rocks near sand. The worms are dependent on sand to build their own tubes. Close inspection of a tube will reveal how it is built up from tiny sand grains.

Each worm has a crown of feeding tentacles that emerge when they are covered by water. These tentacles are deep red or purplish in color, and catch tiny particles suspended in water, including grains of sand. When the tentacles are withdrawn, the food is eaten, and the best sand grains are put to good use in extending the home. When the tide is out, a dark operculum shuts the worm off from the outside world. The Scaly Worm Shell and Red Tube Worm both resemble an individual Sand Castle Worm, but neither of them are made up from sand grains.

OTHER NAME: Honeycomb Worm

RANGE: Southern and Central California

ZONE: middle to lower intertidal; subtidal to 240 ft

HABITATS: attached to rocks near sand

LENGTH: individual to 2 in; colony to 6 feet

COLOR: sandy structure; red or purple worm

SIMILAR SPECIES: Red Tube Worm (p. 173)

Giant Feather Duster
EUDISTYLIA POLYMORPHA

I t is hard to believe, but this beautiful crown of feathers is, in fact, part of a worm. Peer over the edge of a wharf in a clean harbor, and you are sure to see some of these Giant Feather Dusters attached to pilings or submerged wood. These creatures also hang from the sides of surge channels, and can be witnessed in their full glory in rocky tidepools. Some are deeply embedded in crevices, so that the long tube is almost invisible, while others grow in small groups and the long tubes can be very obvious. Inside this tube, the body of the worm is protected.

The feathery feeding apparatus is often red, but can be tan, orange, brown and sometimes banded. This apparatus filters small particles from the water, as well as absorbs oxygen to breathe. Giant Feather Dusters are sensitive creatures, and a gentle touch to their feathery appendages will result in a speedy withdrawal deep into their tube. The crown is about 3 inches in diameter, and emerges from a tube that can be as much as 11 inches long, but seldom is all of the tube seen.

RANGE: Southern California to Alaska

ZONE: lower intertidal; subtidal to 1400 ft

HABITATS: bays; harbors; pilings; open coast; surge channels; tidepools

LENGTH: tube to 11 in

DIAMETER: crown to 3 in

COLOR: tan, red, orange, brown; sometimes banded

SIMILAR SPECIES: Ostrich Plume Hydroid (p. 179)

Kelp Encrusting Bryozoan

MEMBRANIPORA MEMBRANACEA

Storm-tossed kelp might not be the first place you would think to look for mysterious marine organisms, but be sure to pick through some Bull Kelp (p. 188) or Giant Perennial Kelp (p. 187) anyway. Closely hugging the surface of the algae, you might find distinctive pale, delicate mats—lacy filigrees of calcareous walls surrounding hundreds of tiny organisms. These are the Kelp Encrusting Bryozoans. Bryozoans come in so many shapes and sizes—some resembling mossy mats, others looking like branching corals.

Each white patch is a whole colony of animals that resemble miniature anemones, with their circular hand of food-catching tentacles. Tiny walls house and separate each individual bryozoan, and the colony expands from the middle outwards, often giving them a round formation. Close inspection in a tub of water with a hand lens is worthwhile, because the tiny creatures will emerge from their protective homes to feed. Look out for a small patch of jelly-like substance that matches the bryozoan colors perfectly—you might be looking at the 0.6-inch-long Doridella Sea Slug (*Doridella steinbergae*), which browses exclusively on this bryozoan.

OTHER NAME: Lacy-crust Bryozoan

RANGE: Southern California to Alaska

ZONE: subtidal

HABITATS: kelp

LENGTH: colony variable to several inches

COLOR: white, cream, gray

Rosy Bryozoan
EURYSTOMELLA BILABIATA

There are many different kinds of animals and algae that creep, spread and grow on rocks to form carpets and encrustations. It is a challenge trying to determine just what one is, even for the most knowledgeable of scientists, so do not despair! One such organism that you might come across, and might be able to identify, is the Rosy Bryozoan. This encrustation is pinkish or red, often blotched with brown, and where the tiny organisms have died, the bryozoan can be covered with small green algae.

RANGE: Southern California to Alaska

ZONE: middle to low intertidal

HABITATS: rocks

LENGTH: colony variable to several inches

COLOR: pink, red, brown

Rosy Bryozoan colonies start off very small, and gradually spread out from the central point, usually resulting in a roughly circular formation. This bryozoan develops with a typical pattern that is governed by the positioning of each individual organism in its walled home. This pattern is often described as a basket-weave. One of the most rewarding features of these lovely encrustations is not the bryozoan itself, but the potential to find the exquisite pink Hopkin's Rose (p. 120) that almost exclusively lives, feeds and breeds on this bryozoan.

Ostrich Plume Hydroid

AGLAOPHENIA LATIROSTRIS

W hile inspecting the walls and overhangs of surge channels on exposed rocky shores, you might find the feathery colonies of the Ostrich Plume Hydroid. Keep an eye open for the rising tide though, because surge channels are very dangerous places. These hydroids are cnidarians, and are closely related to the anemones, although they certainly don't look related. Each colony consists of a number of stems that have many branches. Examine these branches closely, with a hand lens, and on each branch you should be able to make out individual hydroids in a neat line. Rings of tentacles on each hydroid catch tiny organisms and particles on which the hydroids feed.

RANGE: Southern California to Alaska

ZONE: middle to low intertidal; subtidal

HABITATS: overhangs; surge channels; rocky shores

LENGTH: each 'feather' to 4 in

COLOR: variable, reddish

SIMILAR SPECIES: Giant Feather Duster (p. 176)

Spend some time poking around these feathery bunches because, with a bit of detective work you might stumble across one of the peculiar Smooth Skeleton Shrimps (p. 165). These shrimps dine on the hydroids, and are often well camouflaged amidst the tangle of hydroid branches. If you are nosing around in red Ostrich Plume Hydroids, then expect to find red shrimp. Don't confuse these feathery hydroids with the Giant Feather Duster, which is actually a worm.

Purple Sponge

HALICLONA PERMOLLIS

Soft, smooth and purple, these sponges don't appear to be animals, but they are, albeit primitive. The gorgeously colored Purple Sponge is found encrusting hard surfaces in calmer waters and tidepools. Close inspection will reveal tiny holes in the surface. The really small holes are incurrent holes, inside of which are small cells with beating flagella on them that draw in water. The large holes, which resemble volcanoes, are called 'oscula,' and it is from these that the water flows out.

Sponges are not the most dynamic of animals, their attractive colors being one of the few things that make them stand out. What they do is limited to pumping water through the extensive matrix, sifting the water for microscopic particles on which they dine. The matrix is supported by tiny spicules made of silica, or glass, and hungry sea slugs put these to use in their own skin. One such hungry sea slug is the Ring-spotted Doris (p. 114). The similar gray-green Crumb-of-bread Sponge (*Halichondria panicea*) has a texture resembling bread, and is found in the same range.

RANGE: Southern California to Alaska

ZONE: middle to lower intertidal; subtidal to 20 ft

HABITATS: hard surfaces; protected shores

DIAMETER: to 36 in

COLOR: pink to purple

Velvety Red Sponge

OPHLITASPONGIA PENNATA

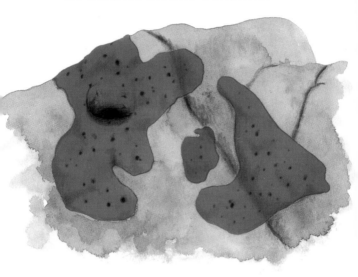

Vibrant dashes of red splashed about on rocks are most likely the brilliant Velvety Red Sponge. This common sponge prefers the open coasts, but seeks out overhangs and darker crevices. Encrusting and very flat, it occurs from the middle intertidal zone down to subtidal waters. As its name implies, it is soft and velvety to the touch and tiny pores pockmark its entire surface.

Get down on your hands and knees to observe the sponge closely, because like most large patches, it is guarding a little secret. As illustrated, you might be able to make out the tiny and adorable Crimson Doris (*Rostanga pulchra*). This sea slug matches the sponge's color to perfection, thus making it hard to notice. The little slug seldom wanders from the sponge that it feeds on and lays eggs on—if it did the slug would become obvious because of its dazzling color. The Crimson Doris barely grows to half an inch in length. Eggs, also bright red, are laid in little coils on the sponge.

RANGE: Southern California to British Columbia

ZONE: middle intertidal; shallow subtidal

HABITATS: rocks; dark crevices; open coasts

DIAMETER: to 36 in

COLOR: red

Sea Pork

APLIDIUM CALIFORNICUM

For those with a bit of imagination, colonies of these encrusting animals might look like a slab of pork. Sea Pork is actually a low-growing mass of tunicates, or sea squirts. These organisms are filter feeders, with an intake and outlet for water to pass through, and they favor very clean water. Where wave action is strong, it is possible to see these creatures. Sea squirts come in various shapes and sizes, and the Sea Pork is a colonial form, of which there are many different species determined in part by their color. Sea Porks usually come in pinkish hues, but white and brown are common shades.

RANGE: Southern California to Alaska

ZONE: lower intertidal; subtidal to 1200 ft

HABITATS: wave-washed rocks; open coasts

DIAMETER: to 8 in

COLOR: variable, white, pink, brown

These colonies are smooth to the touch, and resemble some sponges, but there the similarity ends. Sea squirts are sophisticated equivalents of sponges, but are not related to them. Many animals dine on tunicates, especially snails like the Chestnut Cowry (p. 83) as well as many of the nudibranchs. Food for the Sea Pork is the microscopic component of the water that it filters—bacteria and single-celled plants and animals.

Monterey Stalked Tunicate

STYELA MONTEREYENSIS

This tunicate is distinctive for its long stalk and tough body, with two valves, or siphons, at the top. It is a solitary tunicate, unlike the large colonies of Sea Pork (p. 182) or Yellow-green Sea Squirt (p. 184), and it can often be found suspended from overhangs in quieter corners of surge channels. The protected side of rocks on exposed coasts is favored, and pilings where the water is clean might harbor several individuals. The main body of the animal is wrinkled longitudinally, and the texture is tough and almost woody. The color varies from yellowish to red-brown. Sometimes the tunicate is covered with other organisms, although this seldom happens when it is growing where there are swift currents.

Surprisingly, we have quite a lot in common with sea squirts. A free-swimming larval tunicate has a primitive spinal cord, a stomach and a heart, and is not unlike a human when first developing. As they age, though, this resemblance fades and the cord disappears. As the larva grows, it decides to settle down on a rock, taking on its new adult form.

OTHER NAME: Stalked Sea Squirt

RANGE: Southern California to British Columbia

ZONE: lower intertidal; subtidal to 100 ft

HABITATS: surge channels; rocks; open and protected coasts; pilings

LENGTH: to 10 in

COLOR: tan to red-brown

183

Yellow-green Sea Squirt

CIONA INTESTINALIS

Clean harbors with wooden pilings are wonderful places to catch a glimpse of the marine world. Peek over the edge of a wharf to see all the growth on the wood, and you are more than likely to encounter the Yellow-green Sea Squirt. These tunicates can grow to 6 inches in height and are usually yellowish-green. Their translucent bodies let light pass through to the organs inside—these are faintly visible. Older tunicates are often covered with other marine growths.

OTHER NAME: Sea Vase

RANGE: Southern California to Alaska

ZONE: lower intertidal; subtidal to 1650 ft

HABITATS: rocky areas; pilings; clean harbors; under floats, including boats

HEIGHT: to 6 in

COLOR: translucent yellow-green

The sea squirt has two openings to the body, each one fringed in bright yellow. One of these openings sucks water in, while the other passes it out. This way the Yellow-green Sea Squirt can filter as much as 6 gallons of seawater in a day. Doing so, provides it with oxygen to breathe and with tiny food particles that are suspended in the water. This tunicate often grows in large colonies, frequently carpeting the underside of floating objects, including boats in harbors. A smaller paler sea squirt that resembles a lightbulb is often found in colonies. This one is the Lightbulb Tunicate (*Clavelina huntsmani*), which prefers the open coast.

Feather Boa

EGREGIA MENZIESII

This exotic-looking brown alga is a common kelp of the exposed and semi-protected coasts from Southern California northwards. One of the largest intertidal brown algae, it grows to impressive lengths. It is noticeable for its many small blades (to 2 inches in length) growing off the side of the main stem, or stipe. Some of these blades are enlarged into bulbous floats. The illustration shows just one small portion of a long blade. The upper section of the main blade is a golden-brown, while other parts can be olive-green to dark brown.

RANGE:	Southern California to British Columbia
ZONE:	lower intertidal; shallow subtidal
HABITATS:	rocky shores
LENGTH:	to 15 ft
WIDTH:	to 6 in
COLOR:	olive-green to dark brown

The Shield-backed Kelp Crab (p. 150) often makes its home here, and takes on brown coloration to match the kelp. In addition, a small limpet, less than an inch in length, lives on the stipe and is found nowhere else. This limpet (*Lottia insessa*) is brown and leaves small depressions in the main stem. Feather Boa is common in California, but starts to become scarcer from Oregon northwards. On farms this kelp has often been used as a rich mulch, rivaling manure.

Oar Weed Kelp
LAMINARIA DENTIGERA

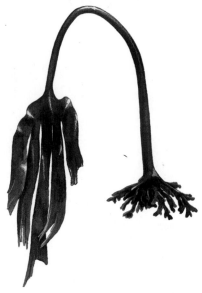

When the tide is at its lowest, groves of Oar Weed Kelp can be seen poking through the water, looking abandoned by the sea. The strong stipes, to 2 feet in length, stick up while supporting a tattered, drooping blade. When the strong waves of the rocky coasts return, they give the standing kelp bed a strong thrashing, allowing the rubbery qualities of the kelp to demonstrate their toughness.

The Oar Weed Kelp grows in surge channels where the surf comes pounding in. In such rough conditions, the blade of the kelp splits many times, which gives it a tattered appearance. Come the year's end, these blades are lost, but the stipe remains and will soon produce another blade. Blades of this brown alga can be as wide as 18 inches, and the whole kelp might reach lengths of 5 feet or more. There are several similar kelps in the genus of *Laminaria*. Another brown alga that can be seen drooping from an erect stipe along the low-tide line is the Southern Sea Palm (*Eisenia arborea*).

RANGE: Southern and Central California

ZONE: lower intertidal; shallow subtidal

HABITATS: exposed, rocky shores; surge channels

LENGTH: to 5 ft

WIDTH: blade to 18 in

COLOR: dark brown, olive-green

Giant Perennial Kelp

MACROCYSTIS SPP.

Giant forests of kelp lie just offshore on the open coast where the surf is not too strong. A huge ball of a holdfast ties their great length (to 40 feet) down to the seafloor. The stem branches many times, each ending with a series of slim blades. The uppermost section of a kelp frond is illustrated (above), and shows the tapered blades with their bulbous bases. These bulbs are gas-filled, which keeps the kelp near the water surface. The grooved blades, to 2 feet in length, are a deep greenish-brown, with toothed edges. New leaf-like blades form by the topmost blade, splitting in half repeatedly.

RANGE: Southern California to Alaska
ZONE: low-tide line; subtidal to 33 ft
HABITATS: rocky shores
LENGTH: to 40 ft
COLOR: dark greenish-brown

The kelp forest's immense productivity is harvested off some coasts—but only the top 3 feet are taken, allowing the kelp to continue growing. This kelp produces 'algin,' a substance with many uses, such as giving ice cream the texture we all love. Storms also take their usual cut of weaker kelp, casting them up in huge piles of wrack. Refer to the Sea Otter (p. 31) for a story about the past demise of these great forests.

Bull Kelp
NEREOCYSTIS LUETKEANA

Bull Kelps have some impressive statistics, growing up to 80 feet long and secured by a massive holdfast that is as much as 16 inches across. Storms toss their distinctive form up on shores where beachcombers are enthralled by them. Because Bull Kelps are scarce south of Point Conception, you could be looking at the very similar Elk Kelp (*Pelagophycus porra*) instead. This kelp has two stems that grow from the float, giving rise to spread-out blades, while Bull Kelp blades arise directly from the float in two clusters.

OTHER NAME: Bull Whip

RANGE: Southern California to Alaska

ZONE: shallow subtidal

HABITATS: exposed, rocky shores

LENGTH: to 80 ft

COLOR: dark greenish-brown

The large, bulbous float is up to 4.5 inches in diameter. This thick-walled vessel is filled with gas and keeps the lengthy fronds afloat. At low tide, they can be seen just off-shore, bobbing in the gentle waves. The tough, hollow stipes take months to rot, and have been used as fishing line. The dark greenish-brown blades grow off two nodes on the float, and reach the length of 10 feet. Stranded stipes, when sliced and pickled, are excellent to eat.

Rockweed
PELVETIA FASTIGIATA

Anyone clambering about the rocks when the tide is out will have come across the successful Rockweeds. Thick, drooping clumps hang down from the tops of intertidal rocks in shades of olive-green to yellowish-green; they are almost black when they dry out. These algae are members of the brown algae family, despite having greenish tones! A shoot grows from a tiny holdfast and then repeatedly divides. At the end of each branch is a swollen 'receptacle' where sex cells are produced. These receptacles are inflated, and when slightly dry, pop and explode under foot.

RANGE: California
ZONE: upper to middle intertidal
HABITATS: rocky shores
LENGTH: to 12 in
COLOR: olive-green, yellowish-green

Walking over rocks covered in this seaweed is hazardous—it produces slimy mucus to keep itself from drying out, but the mucus is devilishly slippery. Be sure to lift up the dangling fronds when beachcombing: it is very moist underneath and all kinds of organisms will be taking refuge here while the tide is out. Figuring out which Rockweed is which is challenging, because there are several different species. This one has thin, rounded stipes that repeatedly divide until they end in the swollen receptacle. For simplicity, only one species is included in this book.

Sargassum
SARGASSUM MUTICUM

Sargassum is easy to identify because of its golden-brown color and tiny, leaf-like blades. Each plant can be over 6 feet in length. These plants float very well with their numerous small, bulbous floats tucked in amongst the blades, which are less than inch long. The Sargassum's success at floating probably explains how this seaweed has now become the established seaweed of California. First introduced from Japan into Puget Sound, Washington, it has spread both up and down the coast, and can now be found in many of the calm-water bays and lagoons of Southern California.

RANGE: Southern California to British Columbia

ZONE: lower intertidal; shallow subtidal

HABITATS: calm water; bays; lagoons; often cast ashore

LENGTH: to 6 ft

COLOR: golden-brown

There are several species of Sargassum to be found, and these usually require close inspection to tell them apart. This intertidal species is related to the open ocean seaweed of the famous Sargasso Sea, usually a calm sea in the Atlantic Ocean where there are gentle currents coming in, but none going out. Thus everything that arrives, stays. Here, there are huge permanent drifts of seaweed harboring their own unique collection of organisms, including unusual crabs and fishes that try to resemble the golden-brown seaweed fronds.

Tar Spot
RALFSIA PACIFICA

It's hard to believe that these encrusting dark brown or black spots are another species of brown alga—they are so easy to step over and ignore. They form thin, encrusting growths on rocks of the middle to lower intertidal zone. Most Tar Spots take on a circular shape, gradually growing outwards. Close inspection of the surface might reveal tiny lines radiating from the central point, as well as concentric ridges. Even under a microscope, it is hard to believe that this organism is really an alga. It is composed of thin layers of cells and tiny threads, all packed in with a tough coat.

RANGE: Southern California to Alaska

ZONE: middle to lower intertidal

HABITATS: rocky shores

DIAMETER: to 8 in

COLOR: dark brown, black

SIMILAR SPECIES: Blobs of Tar (p. 202)

These algae are highly tolerant of extreme conditions. Their dark colors ensure that they absorb most of the sun's radiation, and they become very hot. A tough outer coating helps protect them. Other species of similar encrusting algae can be encountered in shades of red and brown. This one might easily be mistaken for the aftermath of an oil spill, but rest assured, this time it is an alga!

Sea Staghorn
CODIUM FRAGILE

This distinctive green alga is often seen perched on the top or sides of rocks. It is a very dark green, almost black, and the velvety texture feels more like a sponge. From a small holdfast, columnar branches grow, and these branches repeatedly divide in two, giving that antler-like quality. The branches are firm and rounded, standing upright when young. As they grow longer, they droop with their own weight. A dusting of white occurs on some branches.

RANGE: Southern California to Alaska

ZONE: middle to lower intertidal; shallow subtidal

HABITATS: rocky shores

LENGTH: to 16 in

COLOR: very dark green

On close inspection, you might notice the sea slug *Elysia hedgpethi* that lives on this alga. The green pigment (chlorophyll) that the sea slug swallows while eating the alga continues to photosynthesize for some time, perhaps offering sugary nutrition to the slug. The alga is highly nutritious, loaded with vitamins and iron. In Japan it is sugared and eaten as a delicacy, or used in soups and as a garnish. Loved in Japan, it is hated by the fisheries of the East Coast—shellfish bind to it readily, and then the alga breaks off in storms, losing the valuable crop to the sea.

Enteromorpha Green Algae

ENTERMORPHA SPP.

Pools along the highest splash-line of the waves are not easy places to live in. Filled with rainwater one minute and engulfed in sea spray the next, these pools also bear the brunt of the beating sun. One group of algae, Enteromorpha Green Algae, thrives under these trying conditions, and does well enough that whole pools can be filled with their dazzling green tangles. Tubular strands of these algae can be seen along seepages in the cliffs, on mud flats and in estuaries—most often where fresh water and seawater mix.

The fragile strands often fill with bubbles of oxygen, making them float on the surface of the pools. Several forms of these algae occur, all bright green or yellow-green and with either long, thin tubes or flattened, wider strands. When they die, they lose the green chlorophyll pigments and turn a ghostly white. Found worldwide, many cultures eat these algae because they are highly nutritious. If you are tempted, be very cautious—these highly tolerant algae frequently grow in polluted water.

OTHER NAME: Confetti

RANGE: Southern California to Alaska

ZONE: above high-tide line; spray or splash

HABITATS: spraypools; brackish-water seepages; estuaries; mud flats

LENGTH: to 10 in

COLOR: brilliant green, yellow-green

SIMILAR SPECIES: Sea Lettuce (p. 194)

Sea Lettuce

ULVA LACTUCA

Bright green and frilled, this alga has earned the name 'Sea Lettuce.' It is edible and eaten as a rich source of vitamins and minerals in some parts of the world. The blades of the alga are only two cells thick, and are consequently translucent. When the oblong sheets dry out, they crinkle. The Sea Lettuce attaches to rocks from the upper to lower intertidal zone, but is confined to tidepools in the upper intertidal zone. It can be seen gently drifting on mud flats and in estuaries, bays and lagoons.

RANGE: Southern California to Alaska

ZONE: upper to lower intertidal

HABITATS: rocky shores; tidepools; calm waters

LENGTH: to 20 in

COLOR: bright green

SIMILAR SPECIES: Enteromorpha Green Algae (p. 193)

There are several species of *Ulva*, or maybe not—biologists have yet to decide just how many we are dealing with. Some species come as uniform sheets, while others are perforated with holes and have tatty edges. The Sea Lettuce turns up on other seaweeds and occasionally on the backs of shells. If the water has gone green in a tidepool, this alga has released its tiny reproductive cells from the edges of its blades. Equally as green, Enteromorpha Green Algae grow as fine strands.

Nail Brush

ENDOCLADIA MURICATA

This common alga has predominantly red pigments and appears dark red to purple, sometimes brown. It favors the very high reaches of the shore, where it clings to the rocks in the close company of hardy Acorn Barnacles (p. 158). Here, it is exposed to the rigors of intertidal life, drying up in hot sunshine. As it dries out, the colors become very dark, almost black, and the thin branches shrivel. When wet it is soft and supple, but when dry it is coarse and wiry.

OTHER NAME: Sea Moss
RANGE: Southern California to Alaska
ZONE: upper intertidal
HABITATS: rocky shores
LENGTH: to 3 in
COLOR: dark red, purple, black

Little clumps, resembling woodland moss, scatter the rocks of exposed and partially protected shores. These are hardy tufts of algae, some of which might not feel the spray of the ocean for more than a day, because they grow so high in the intertidal zone. The fine texture is made from many slender branches, each of which is covered by tiny spines. These dense little forests are well worth poking into, because many tiny creatures crawl inside the tangle to take shelter from predators and the elements.

Turkish Towel
GIGARTINA EXASPERATA

Turkish Towel is an attractive addition to rocky and cobble shores, where its splashes of red add to the browns and greens in the mats of seaweed. Brightly colored when young, this seaweed becomes a very dark purple-red, losing its brilliance, and sometimes appearing almost black as it ages. The blades are long and wide, and covered in small nodules that give this species a rough texture like a coarse towel. When submerged or very wet, the blades have an iridescent bluish sheen. There are many flat, bladed red algae, and this algae is one of the easiest to identify.

RANGE: Southern California to British Columbia

ZONE: lower intertidal; subtidal to 60 ft

HABITATS: rocky shores; cobble shores

LENGTH: to 18 in

WIDTH: to 10 in

COLOR: bright red to very dark purple-red

Several species of *Gigartina* grow on our shores. They are only obvious in summer when the blades rapidly expand from small growths on the holdfast. In winter, the blades die off and are a frequent addition to the wrack left on the beaches after a storm. The little holdfast sits tight through winter, waiting for spring and new growth. Turkish Towels are an excellent source of 'carrageenan,' an agent that is used in industry and foods for many different applications.

Iridescent Seaweed

IRIDAEA CORDATA

This very attractive seaweed is deep red overlaid with an iridescence that gives tints of purple, blue and green to the fleshy and slippery, smooth blade. A newcomer to this alga would be forgiven for thinking that the oily sheen was from the aftermath of an oil spill—this phenomenon is entirely the product of nature. From a small holdfast comes one dominant blade, with several smaller blades beside. The edges undulate and are often torn by the action of the waves. The very young blades are blue. In winter they die back, leaving the sturdy holdfast from which new blades will grow the following spring. There are many different species of red seaweeds with thin, red blades found on the rocky shores, and this species is one of the most distinctive. It is common north of Santa Barbara.

RANGE: from Santa Barbara north to Alaska
ZONE: lower intertidal; shallow subtidal
HABITATS: rocky shores
LENGTH: to 36 in
COLOR: deep red; iridescent

Like the Turkish Towel (p. 196), Iridescent Seaweed is loaded with carrageenan. Research is underway to establish profitable and practical ways to commercially grow this alga, perhaps offering a way of growing the seaweed without having to pillage the shores for it.

Coralline Algae
CORALLINA SPP.

Carpets of Coralline Algae coat the bottom and sides of some tidepools. Where other seaweeds get chewed to bits, these tough ones are left alone; the tidepool residents just don't enjoy them. Although often feathery in appearance, these algae have a very tough texture that results from heavily calcified walls. Cells deposit so much lime (calcium carbonate) that early naturalists thought they were studying a type of coral animal and not a plant!

Bright pink to deep purple, the fronds are often edged in white. These jointed branches arise from a flat, encrusting growth spreading over the rock. Most of the alga is rigid, but at the joints there is less lime, so some flexibility is the result. This pliancy is an advantage when the rough surf crashes in. Many different species of Coralline Algae never grow to more than a few inches in length. When they die, they rapidly bleach white. While most Coralline Algae avoid being eaten because of their toughness, some Coralline Algae grow as encrustations that might be grazed by some snails and chitons.

RANGE: Southern California to Alaska

ZONE: lower intertidal; shallow subtidal

HABITATS: rocky shores; open coasts

LENGTH: to 4 in

COLOR: bright pink to dark purple

Encrusting Coral

LITHOTHAMNIUM PACIFICUM

Often overlooked, these pretty crusts are not strange rocks, but algae related to Coralline Algae (p. 198). Forming small patches of tough growths, Encrusting Coral might merge to create large colonies, overlapping and growing on top of one another. Usually pink, this alga also comes in deep purple, and the edges or nodules on its surface might be fringed in white. An encrusting resident of rocks, it will also grow on shells and is commonly seen near the low-tide line, especially in tidepools.

OTHER NAME:	Pink Rock Crusts
RANGE:	Southern California to British Columbia
ZONE:	low-tide line; shallow subtidal
HABITATS:	rocks; shells; tidepools
DIAMETER:	variable to several inches
COLOR:	white, pink, purple

Many patches have knobs on the surface and small, white dots might be evident. It is from these dots that microscopic spores emerge to start new encrustations. The crustiness of this alga is attributed to the heavy deposits of lime (calcium carbonate) that it extracts from seawater. Despite being so hard, it does fall prey to some mollusks. The White-cap Limpet (p. 52) lives on it, and is frequently overgrown with it, and the extravagantly marked Lined Chiton (p. 109) adheres to it, grazing slowly and adopting pinkish coloration to blend in with the alga.

Surf Grass

PHYLLOSPADIX SPP.

On rocky shores, huge beds of Surf Grass sway back and forth with the wash of waves. These vivid green leaves are not those of algae, but rather of flowering plants, just like some relatives on land. They have a root system, instead of a holdfast, and require sediment to sink their roots into. The leaves are long, slim and a brilliant green, and the flowers are nestled tightly against the stems.

RANGE: Southern California to Alaska

ZONE: middle to lower intertidal

HABITATS: rocky shores; open coasts

LENGTH: to 36 in

COLOR: green

SIMILAR SPECIES: Eelgrass (p. 201)

There are two common species of Surf Grass that are essentially similar.

Surf Grass beds are excellent habitats to poke around in. A small isopod (*Idotea montereyensis*), resembling Harford's Greedy Isopod (p. 166), clings to the leaves and matches the green color. Shield-backed Kelp Crabs (p. 150) can also be seen tenaciously grasping with their long legs, as the leaves sway back and forth, and some thick beds of Surf Grass are a favored hiding place for various crabs and lobsters at low tide. Sometimes, the vivid green color is masked by an excessive growth of a fuzzy, red alga, *Smithora naiadum*. Surf Grass resembles the Eelgrass of calmer sandy waters.

Eelgrass
ZOSTERA MARINA

Don some waders and be sure to gently walk through the extensive Eelgrass meadows of quiet bays. Eelgrass prefers water with a gentle flow, where some fresh water has mixed with the sea. Like Surf Grass, which it resembles, Eelgrass is a flowering plant. The green leaves are strap-like, with inconspicuous flowers tucked near the stems. Eelgrass spreads through muddy sand with rooty rhizomes from which new plants grow.

The thick mat of Eelgrass stabilizes the soft mud, and is easy to walk on. The meadows are rewarding for beachcombers because of the diverse wildlife they harbor. These meadows are perfect nurseries for young fishes and crabs, such as the Shield-backed Kelp Crab (p. 150). Anemones wave their tentacles, while snails graze upon all kinds of encrustations and smother the leaves and stems. Nudibranchs creep about and pulsing jellyfish drift by. Shrimp dart around your feet. Clams have siphons peeking above the muddy surface, and sea stars cruise along the bottom in search of prey. A meadow of Eelgrass is wildlife at your feet, and you don't have to watch out for dangerous waves!

RANGE: Southern California to Alaska

ZONE: lower intertidal; shallow subtidal

HABITATS: quiet bays; muddy or sandy bottoms

LENGTH: to 36 in

COLOR: green

SIMILAR SPECIES: Surf Grass (p. 200)

Blobs of Tar

HOMINIS POLLUTANTISSIMUM

Beachcombing does come with minor hazards. Watch out for Blobs of Tar! These globular, black masses hide in sand, or stick to rocks. Try to avoid them if you can, because they are sticky and hard to remove. Get some on your skin and you will be scrubbing like crazy. Get some on your clothes and you might as well throw them away. Blobs of Tar can be tenacious and long lasting. Don't confuse them with the all-natural algal Tar Spots.

Unfortunately, our beautiful oceans suffer from human activity in many ways. Blobs of Tar are tiny versions of larger problems—oil slicks. Tankers have accidents, and oil, in its various forms, pours onto the oceans, sticking to the feathers of birds and the soft fur of otters. These animals get waterlogged and die. Fish and shellfish suffocate, and many creatures are slowly poisoned. Oil is just one example of our neglect of the oceans. So remember that the oceans are sacred and think about your actions when you visit. Respect all wildlife and water, and please take all that garbage home with you.

RANGE: Southern California to Alaska

ZONE: upper to lower intertidal; inshore; offshore

HABITATS: indiscriminate

LENGTH: microscopic to miles

COLOR: usually oily black

SIMILAR SPECIES: Tar Spot (p. 191)

Glossary

anal fin
the fin running underneath the fish behind the anus, but in front of the tail

aperture
the opening to the shell of gastropods out of which the animal emerges

bivalve
group of mollusks possessing two valves or shells that enclose the animal

byssal threads
tough threads made of strong protein secreted by some bivalves to attach themselves firmly to rocks

calcareous
whitish deposits or material made from calcium carbonate (lime), like shells

calcium carbonate
white, hard compound extracted from the sea to make shells, also called lime

carapace
large, flat portion of the crab's shell covering the head and thorax from which the legs arise; often washed ashore after molting

carnivore
consumes other animals or parts of them

cerata
fleshy growths on the back of some nudibranchs, usually with an extension of the gut running inside

cirrus
hand-like appendages, or small, hairy growths; used in reference to growths on fish heads and the feathery feet of barnacles for filter feeding

commensal
where one organism lives with, in or on another, gaining some advantages such as food or shelter, without harming its host

crustacean
group of arthropods, including the crabs, shrimp and beach fleas

encrustation
usually a low, flat, firm growth (crust) covering a surface

GLOSSARY

estuarine
where a fresh-water river exits into the sea; salinity drops because the salts are diluted by the fresh water, and both sea and river influence local geography

filter feeder
an organism that feeds using feathered or net-like appendages, or other means, to extract tiny or even microscopic particles suspended in the water

gastropod
molluskan snails, such as whelks, dogwinkles and limpets

girdle
fleshy band surrounding the plates of chitons

herbivore
consumes plants or parts of plants

holdfast
root-like structure with which seaweeds attach themselves to rocky substrates

intertidal zone
zone between low-tide line and high-tide line

mantle
sheet of living tissue that secretes the shells of snails and encloses the delicate gills

midrib
central rib running the length of some blades of kelp (absent in other species)

nematocyst
specialized stinging cells found in the tentacles of jellyfishes, anemones and corals

nocturnal
active by night

nudibranch
another name for sea slug

omnivore
consumes pretty much anything it wants to, provided it is worth it

operculum
a horny door with which a gastropod shuts itself in; used to protect against predators, and to prevent from drying out during low tide

periostracum
tough organic layer on the shell of mollusks

GLOSSARY

plankton
tiny organisms suspended in water drifting at the mercy of the currents and tides

radula
tooth-like structure used for scraping or boring, taking on various forms depending on the diet of the gastropod or chiton

red tide
occasional blooms of a single-celled organism causes reddening of water; toxins from these organisms build up in the flesh of shellfishes; not a toxin you want to consume

rhinophores
sensory structures, like tentacles, on the head of nudibranchs

salinity
level of salt in water; high salinity means lots of sea salt

sessile
sitting, or fixed, usually incapable of moving around, as in the case of barnacles and mussels

silica
hard mineral, like quartz and glass, occurring in sponge spicules

siphons
tube-like extensions from mollusks to obtain water that is drawn into the mantle cavity; particularly evident in burrowing bivalves

stipe
seaweed equivalent of a stem

test
tough supporting structure, or skeleton, of echinoderms, such as the Eccentric Sand Dollars found on beaches

umbo
located near the hinge of bivalve mollusk, is the oldest part of the mollusk, often prominent and beak-like

valve
one half, or shell, of a bivalve

whorl
one complete turn of a spire on a snail shell

zooid
individual member of a bryozoan colony

zooplankton
animal component of plankton (the plant element being phytoplankton)

Further Reading

Behrens, David W. 1980. *Pacific Coast Nudibranchs*. Los Osos, California: Sea Challengers.

Dawson, E. Yale, and Michael S. Foster. 1982. *Seashore Plants of California*. Berkeley: University of California Press.

Delphine, Haley (ed). 1978. *Marine Mammals of the Eastern North Pacific and Arctic Waters*. Seattle, Washington: Pacific Search Press.

Goodson, Car. 1988. *Fishes of the Pacific Coast*. Stanford, California: Stanford University Press.

Gotshall, Daniel W. 1994. *Guide to Marine Invertebrates: Alaska to Baja California*. Monterey, California: Sea Challengers.

Harbo, Rick M. 1997. *Shells and Shellfish of the Pacific Northwest*. Madeira Park, British Columbia: Harbour Publishing.

Hinton, Sam. 1987. *Seashore Life of Southern California*. Berkeley: University of California Press.

Jensen, Gregory C. 1995. *Pacific Coast Crabs and Shrimps*. Monterey, California: Sea Challengers.

Kozloff, Eugene N. 1993. *Seashore Life of the Northern Pacific Coast: An Illustrated Guide to Northern California, Oregon, Washington and British Columbia*. Seattle, Washington: University of Washington Press.

Love, Milton. 1996. *Probably More Than You Want to Know About the Fishes of the Pacific Coast*. Santa Barbara, California: Really Big Press.

McConnaughey, B.H., and E. McConnaughey. 1988. *Pacific Coast*. The Audubon Society Nature Guides. New York: Alfred A. Knopf.

Morris, Percy A. 1980. *Pacific Coast Shells*. Peterson Field Guide Series. Boston, Massachusetts: Houghton Mifflin Company.

Niesen, Thomas M. 1994. *Beachcomber's Guide to California Marine Life*. Houston, Texas: Gulf Publishing Company.

Reish, Donald J. 1995. *Marine Life of Southern California*. Dubuque, Iowa: Kendall/Hunt Publishing Company.

Ricketts, Edward F., and Jack Calvin. 1968. *Between Pacific Tides*. Stanford, California: Stanford University Press.

Waaland, J. Robert. 1977. *Common Seaweeds of the Pacific Coast*. Seattle, Washington: Pacific Search Press.

Index

Page numbers in bold typeface indicate primary, illustrated species.

INDEX

INDEX

INDEX

INDEX

About the Author

Ian Sheldon, an accomplished artist, naturalist and educator, has lived in South Africa, Singapore, Britain and Canada. Caught collecting caterpillars at the age of three, he has been exposed to the beauty and diversity of nature ever since. He was educated at Cambridge University and the University of Alberta. When he is not in the tropics working on conservation projects or immersing himself in our beautiful wilderness, he is sharing his love for nature. Ian enjoys communicating this passion through the visual arts and the written word.

Photograph by Al Day

Ian cavorts with a moonsnail at low tide.

MORE GREAT BOOKS ABOUT THE OUTDOORS

WHALES AND OTHER MARINE MAMMALS OF CALIFORNIA AND BAJA
by Tamara Eder
illustrations by Ian Sheldon
Color photographs and illustrations
8.5" x 5.5" • 176 pages
ISBN13: 978-1-55105-342-4
$12.95

MAMMALS OF CALIFORNIA
by Tamara Eder

Color photographs
and illustrations
8.5" x 5.5" • 344 pages
ISBN13: 978-1-55105-344-8
$22.95

ANIMAL TRACKS OF SOUTHERN CALIFORNIA
by Ian Sheldon

B/W illustrations
5.75" x 4.25" • 176 pages
ISBN13: 978-1-55105-105-5
$6.95

ANIMAL TRACKS OF NORTHERN CALIFORNIA
by Ian Sheldon

B/W illustrations
5.75" x 4.25" • 176 pages
ISBN13: 978-1-55105-103-1
$7.95

BIRDS OF SAN DIEGO
by Chris C. Fisher and Herbert Clarke

Color illustrations
8.5" x 5.5" • 160 pages
ISBN13: 978-1-55105-102-4
$9.95

BIRDS OF LOS ANGELES Including Santa Barbara, Ventura and Orange Counties
by Chris C. Fisher and Herbert Clark
Color illustrations
8.5" x 5.5" • 160 pages
ISBN13: 978-1-55105-104-8
$9.95

WILDFLOWERS OF THE SIERRA NEVADA AND THE CENTRAL VALLEY
by Laird R. Blackwell

450 color photographs
8.5" x 5.5" • 288 pages
ISBN13: 978-1-55105-226-7
$15.95

WILDFLOWERS OF THE TAHOE SIERRA
by Laird R. Blackwell

100 color photographs
6.25" x 4" • 144 pages
ISBN13: 978-1-55105-085-0
$9.95

LONE PINE PUBLISHING

1808 B Street NW, Suite 140
Auburn, Washington 98001
Telephone: 1-800-548-3541

www.lonepinepublishing.com